# SECRETS

## of Golf Instruction and Flexibility

Your Guide to Mastering Golf's TRUE Fundamentals

# SECRETS

## of Golf Instruction and Flexibility

Your Guide to Mastering Golf's TRUE Fundamentals

By
Roger Fredericks

Foreword
by
Arnold Palmer

SECRETS
OF GOLF INSTRUCTION AND FLEXIBILITY.

Library of Congress Control Number: 2010936548

Secrets of Golf Instruction and Flexibility:
Your Guide to Mastering Golf's True Fundamentals
by Roger Fredericks - First Edition

Mountain Lion, Inc.
ISBN 978-0-9770039-5-2

Printed in the United States of America by Lake Book Manufacturing, Inc.
www.LakeBook.com

**Disclaimer**

The information and exercises within this book were designed to educate golfers on the direct relationship between flexibility and its effects on the golf swing, for the purpose of creating a freer and more powerful golf swing. They were not, however, designed to treat specific injuries. Although flexibility exercises can be a great benefit to treating injuries, please consult your health care practitioner before embarking on this or any other program. The instructions and advice presented in this book are in no way intended as a substitute for counseling from your health care professional. The creators, and participants, in this project disclaim any liability of loss in connection with the exercises, instructions, and advice herein.

Photographs within this book include those courtesy of Getty Images, Golf Magazine, Hugh Smith and Scott Miller.

Book Cover Design by Kim Spangle, Spangle Design
Book Design by Jean Fredericks

# Testimonials

"… I am very pleased to see that Roger is now bringing the principles of anatomical function into the golf world, where I believe that they will have a substantial impact on not only your golf swing, but also carry over into your everyday life as well…."

**Jack Nicklaus**
*World Golf Hall of Fame*

"Roger and I adamantly believe, that in order to play great golf one has to be flexible, strong, and eat correctly. If you want a better golf game, Roger's the man to help you."

**Gary Player**
*World Golf Hall of Fame*

"Today there is more understanding of the relationship between being fit and playing good golf. It is difficult to have one without the other. Roger's instruction and stretching exercises will no doubt accelerate your path from "wanting to be a good player" to actually "becoming one."

**Tom Kite**
*World Golf Hall of Fame*

"I honestly believe that Roger's program is the best that I've ever seen for amateurs or pros."

**Donna Caponi**
*World Golf Hall of Fame*

"Roger's program will help you on and off the course, just like it did for me."

**Bernhard Langer**
*World Golf Hall of Fame*

"In this book, Roger reveals the "Secrets" to the game of golf. He has done a great job explaining how your body dictates your performance and how golf [like all sports], requires balance, and how a functional body is the key to executing a fundamental golf swing."

**Pete Egoscue**
*Founder, The Egoscue Method®*
*Author,* **Pain Free** *Book Series*

"Roger's program is the best. If he can take an old guy like me and make me win the Senior PGA at 58, I'll tell you what, his program must work!"

**John Jacobs (J.J.)**
*2003 Senior PGA Champion*

"I now stand up straight, I have great posture, my feet point forward, and I feel wonderful. If you follow what Roger has outlined in this book, you will too!"

**Jim Hardy**
*Top 50 Golf Instructor*
*Author of* **The Plane Truth**

"Roger Fredericks answered all of the 'whys' that I had about my golf swing. After reading this book, you too will finally know why you do what you do in your golf swing, and more importantly, what to do about it."

**John Mahaffey**
*1978 PGA Champion*

"Roger taught me that just because we get older doesn't mean you have to lose your flexibility."

**Tommy Jacobs**
*Former Ryder Cup Member*

"Roger's program will help you get into great shape, just like it did for me."

**Peter Jacobsen**
*2004 Senior U.S. Open Champion*

"Roger's program has helped me regain much of the flexibility that I had in my youth. His program got me hitting the ball as solidly as I ever have from tee to green. He's really on to something!"

**Bob Charles**
*1963 British Open Champion*

"Roger Fredericks' program is on the cutting edge of the future of golf instruction. His programs have helped me on and off the course, and every time I see him, I learn that much more."

**Al Geiberger**
*"Mr. 59"*

"I learned more from Roger Fredericks in the half day that I spent with him than in all the years that I've been playing golf. Within two weeks after going through his program, I drove the ball over 400 yards several times!"

**Doug Miller**
*2006 Senior World Long Drive Champion (360 yards)*


"Roger Fredericks is a great coach who *really* knows the golf swing. Not only is he expert in teaching the golf swing, but also in the biomechanics of the body. I feel fortunate to be one of his students."

**Joe Theismann**
*Former NFL Most Valuable Player*
*Super Bowl Champion*
*Washington Redskins*


"I believe that communication is vital for anyone to be a great coach, and Roger Fredericks is a great communicator. He's the best."

**Mike Shanahan**
*Two-Time Super Bowl Champion Coach*


"Roger will take you on a step-by-step journey into the world of flexibility. If you follow the programs that he's outlined in this book, you'll not only learn the true fundamentals of getting more flexible, but the truth about your own golf swing. Roger is a master of flexibility."

**Dr. Greg Rose**
*Founder Titleist Performance Institute*

"If you need more power and consistency in your golf swing, it may be as simple as your flexibility. In my opinion, there is no one more qualified to teach flexibility for the golf swing than Roger. In this book you will learn the secrets to regaining your flexibility at any age. I know it will help your golf game...and your life."

**Dave Phillips**
*Cofounder Titleist Performance Institute*

"Roger Fredericks is doing golfers of all ilk a great service with his incredible flexibility programs designed for golf. Avail yourself to this book, and you'll be doing yourself a great favor, on and off the course.

**Eddie Merrins**
*Bel Air CC*
*World Golf Teachers Hall of Fame*

"Roger's knowledge of the golf swing and how a person's individual body type affects their golf swing mechanics is second to none. Spending time with him filming his infomercial was an eye opener for me and I'm very pleased that he's now sharing his vast knowledge with the golf world."

**Gary Koch**
*6 Time PGA Tour Winner*
*Television Broadcaster*

"Very few instructors understand the human body and how it works. Not only does Roger understand it, but he can help you gain the flexibility and strength you need to create a more effective golf swing."

**Mike Malaska**
*Golf Magazine & Golf Digest*
*Top 50 Instructors*

# Contents

# Acknowledgements

I have a strong belief that all people are given certain "gifts" by the Creator; gifts that can manifest in an amazing variety of ways. I believe that if there is a secret to life, it just may be for each of us to discover what our individual gifts are and then use them, not only to help us go through life's many twists and turns, but especially to share them with others. I believe that one of the gifts that I've been given is the incredible number of fascinating people and friends—from all walks of life—that have come into and played a role in my life. Unfortunately there are too many people that have influenced me to name here, but I would like to thank the ones who have contributed the most to the creation of this book.

I am especially grateful to David Chapman (my jockey) for believing in my message and putting together the amazing partnership that I have today. David, you are the man! To Charlie Mechem (The Godfather), whose wisdom, counsel and especially friendship, has helped me in more ways than I can express. To Arnold Palmer, for letting me hang out in his "kingdom" and allowing me to see his genius on how to treat people up close.

To Tommy Jacobs, whose friendship and belief in my message set the stage for this book. To Jim Achenbach, for hearing my message and using his professionalism to take the knowledge out of my head and onto these pages. To Ric McDonald and Pete Egoscue, for opening my eyes to a "functional world."

To my mother, Doris Fredericks, whose unshakable and positive personality was felt by all, and my father, Elmer Fredericks, for teaching me to see the truth in all things.

To my wonderful and incredible wife, Jean, my lover and best friend, who always brings me back to seeing things clearly, and to my son, Ryan, for being the inspiration of my life.

And most of all, to the legions of people and students who have certainly taught me far more than I've ever taught them. I thank you all for giving me your gifts.

*Roger Fredericks*

# Foreword

## By
### Arnold Palmer

Early in the week at the 2003 Senior PGA Championship at Aronimink Golf Club, I played a practice round with my long-time friend and fellow tour professional, Tommy Jacobs.

I hadn't played with Tommy for a number of years, but the thing that caught my attention was how far he was hitting his drives. At the time, he was close to 70 years old, and he was, bombing the ball–he was as long as most pros who are 20 years younger. I told Tommy how surprised I was that he hadn't lost any distance, like the rest of us had.

Tommy informed me that he had actually *gained* a lot of distance because he had embarked on a unique flexibility program developed by a PGA professional and fitness expert named Roger Fredericks.

For the next year, it seemed like everywhere I went, Roger's name kept popping up in conversations, as more and more friends and golf professionals had caught wind of his program, and they too were giving testimonials to the great results that his program had given them.

Finally in December of 2004, I was introduced to Roger by my friend David Chapman at a course that I had designed, the Tradition Golf Club in La Quinta, California.

Roger had put together videos of my current golf swing and compared them to my swing as a younger man. Then he ran me through some simple but very revealing flexibility tests, in which, I must admit, I performed poorly. At that point, Roger explained precisely how my lack of flexibility as demonstrated by these tests had directly affected the restrictions that we had just seen in my golf swing. He explained to me, in no uncertain terms, that if I wanted my swing and shoulder turn to be longer, I needed to increase my flexibility. It was that simple.

The most impressive thing about this meeting was that, for the first time, someone was able to answer all of the questions that I had about my golf swing. Roger explained in detail the relationship of the body and the golf swing. It was an eye-opener.

If my lack of flexibility was the bad news, there also was good news. Roger was adamant in his belief that I could regain a tremendous amount of flexibility and radically improve my golf swing if I followed his program diligently. Shortly thereafter, I flew him down to Bay Hill in Orlando, where we started my training in earnest.

I strongly recommend that you follow Roger's instructions in this book, as I am confident that you will experience the amazing benefits that his wonderful program has given to me and thousands of others.

Although Roger has designed this program for golf, there is no doubt that it will also carry over into your life away from the golf course. I only wish I had started it 20 years ago.

I am honored to help Roger promote this powerful message. What we are trying to do, is make the greatest game on Earth even more enjoyable for everyone who plays it.

*Arnold Palmer*

# Prologue
## The 400-Year-Old Mystery

For more than 400 years, the game of golf has been one of the most mysterious and fascinating pursuits ever invented by mankind. From the Scottish sheepherders to modern day athletes, from laborers to executives, from heads of state to the common man, people are fascinated by golf. It seems to seize the imagination and scramble the mind of every person who plays it, or has ever played it. Yet over all these decades, the debate on what is the "right way" or the "best method" to swing a golf club still exists. Thousands of books and magazine articles have been written on the subject. Endless videos have been produced. Many instructors want to provide the secret for improving our golf games. Regardless, there is no conclusive proof that one way is better than another way. There is no compelling evidence that a particular way is absolutely the right way.

Some teachers have told us to turn our hips, while others have told us to quiet our hips. Some have told us to cup our wrists; others have told us to keep them flat. They have told us to swing upright; they have told us to swing on plane. They have told us to keep our elbow in tight; they have told us to let it fly. They have told us to make a big shoulder turn (when most of us have known that we couldn't do it). They have told us this, and they have told us that. But what they seldom tell us is this: despite the remarkable advancements in golf technology, golf instruction, and golf course conditioning, handicaps have scarcely come down over the last 30 years. In other words, the overwhelming majority of golfers haven't improved.

## THERE'S NO ONE RIGHT WAY TO SWING A GOLF CLUB

The truth is obvious: If we take a look at golf's all-time greatest players, it is clear there is no absolute correct way to swing a golf club (*fig* P.1-P.3). There have been great players who played with strong grips, weak grips, neutral grips, crisscross grips, long thumb, short thumb, overlap, interlock, and 10-finger, and even a few gifted players who played with cross-hand grips. There have been players who set the wrists early, players who took the club back in one piece, and players who dragged it back. There have been inside takeaways, straight back takeaways, and outside loopy takeaways.

### WHICH POSITION IS CORRECT?

P.1. Layed Off.

P.2. Down the Line.

P.3. Across the Line.

*Secrets of Golf Instruction and Flexibility*

*Lack of flexibility is the
number one problem in golf.*

There have been upright planes, neutral planes, and flat planes. There have been cupped wrists, flat wrists, and convex wrists. Since there have been great players who played with each one of these characteristics, *who's to say which way is the "right way"?*

## THE GREATEST SECRET NEVER TOLD

Looking at all the swing mechanics and tips that golf instructors are passing along to their students, people have naturally assumed that all golfers can "do it." The truth is that *not* all golfers can "do it." Some can, but many can't. If your body is not flexible enough to accommodate a certain movement, you probably will introduce a compensating swing mistake in your attempt to make that movement.

Most instructors unschooled in flexibility invariably tell their students to "keep working on it." It should be clear that in many cases this is a myth. If everybody could do it, then everybody would be improving—and most people don't improve. The teachers often blame it on lack of practice or poor practice habits, but I'm saying there's another reason.

## THE BIGGEST PROBLEM IN GOLF

Electromyographic research has proven that PGA Tour players possess 50 to 100 percent more flexibility in their upper trunks than average golfers. Furthermore, they possess about a two-thirds faster pelvic rotation through the shot than the average person. There is no doubt in my mind that lack of flexibility is the number one problem in golf. Most golfers, even some with a high degree of skill, are plagued by their inability to move their bodies in an effective and efficient manner. As a result, they are tormented by their failure to achieve prescribed positions in the golf swing.

The cause of this is no mystery. Humans today have lifestyles that are largely sedentary. We sit at our jobs, sit in our cars and sit at home in front of our televisions. As a result, our bodies become anatomically dysfunctional and we then bring these dysfunctional bodies to the golf course. And then we bogey our brains out. All this sitting has weakened some muscles, tightened others, and greatly affected the capacity of many individuals to make a proper golf swing. After all, the golf swing is a complex athletic move. It is gymnastic in its demands on the human body. Most golfers do not possess the flexibility to move their bodies into the positions that their instructors want. They aren't even close. They might as well attempt to stand on their heads while hitting golf shots.

## THE FUTURE OF GOLF INSTRUCTION

Many golf teachers do not recognize the fragile relationship between the human body and the golf swing. If students repeatedly are asked to do things they cannot do, they become frustrated. Often they get angry—with themselves, with their teachers, or with the game of golf itself. No wonder golf has flatlined, with the number of new golfers not matching the number of golfers leaving the game. This frustration is exactly what golf does not need. Golf is supposed to be relaxing. It is supposed to be engrossing. It is supposed to be fun. There is no room for anger.

P.4. 3D motion-capture systems are revealing many truths about what the body is doing during the golf swing motion.

A new era is dawning in golf instruction. I believe that the instructor of the future will recognize how a person's body affects his ability to make a golf swing. The instructor of the future will be an expert in flexibility and athletic training. He will know as much about hip flexors as he does about high fades. He will teach golf, of course, but he also will be expert in flexibility exercises and fitness.

Think about it. Think how diligently you tried to make that shoulder turn or some other move. There might have been a voice inside you that said "This is hard. This doesn't feel good. Am I doing this right?" If so, then perhaps you

*Secrets of Golf Instruction and Flexibility*

should have paid attention to that voice. The answer to this dilemma does not lie only in swing instruction. It also lies in regular flexibility training, followed by some strength and cardiovascular training. What happens to golfers who do not possess the necessary flexibility to perform a fundamental golf swing? The answer is simple: Their bodies always make some kind of compensation in an attempt to rectify this lack of flexibility.

If you can't turn your shoulders properly on the backswing, your body will find a way to compensate by moving other body parts. You might rise up, your rear leg may straighten, or your lower body may slide and lose its stability. You might feel as if you are doing it right, but video analysis and especially 3D motion-capture systems (*fig* P.4) always expose the truth. Compensations in the golf swing invariably lead to a loss of stability at some point during the swing. Lose your stability and your center of balance and you have lost the war to the golf demons.

Flexibility is the answer. Flexibility will lead to a sound, repeatable golf swing. This book is all about incorporating sound golf instruction principles with flexibility training exercises. The intent is to solidify the instruction by making it easier to perform the movements.

## THE GOOD NEWS
The good news is that everybody, no matter what their age, can improve the range of motion in their bodies by stretching the right muscles in the right way. When we improve the range of motion in our bodies, we automatically improve the range of motion in our swings—pure and simple.

*You don't have to lose flexibility as you get older. In fact, you can gain a considerable amount of flexibility if you do the right stretches the right way.*

I incorporated these principles into my own life more than 20 years ago, and they have literally transformed my body and my golf swing. Now at age 59, I am more flexible than I ever was in my teens, 20s, or 30s. Believe me when I say this: You don't have to lose flexibility as you get older. In fact, you can gain a considerable amount of flexibility if you do the right stretches the right way.

During the last two decades, I have exposed thousands of people to these principles and have received great joy from watching them reconstruct their bodies and their golf swings. They have rediscovered a fountain of youth if you will. It is my goal to redirect the thinking of the legions of golfers who play this wonderful game and help them realize the potential and joy that dwells within them.

You *can* make a bigger shoulder turn, you *can* learn to control your body, and you *can* increase your flexibility. In addition, you *can* realize the greatest gift that any golfer can ever receive—a freer and more powerful golf swing. I know you can do this because I see people improve every day at my golf instruction schools.

# My Story

**Y**ou must have one heck of a sore left ankle when you hit a lot of golf balls." Those words were uttered to me in 1985 by a physical therapist named Ric McDonald, who at the time was the head trainer for the San Diego Chargers football team. Although I didn't know it at the time, that one sentence would change the course of my life and would actually start me out on a new career.

That sentence became so important to me that it is etched in my memory. Ric said it just as I was about to put my hand on the doorknob and leave his office. We had just concluded a business meeting that had nothing to do with physical therapy or golf. Flabbergasted, I turned to him and asked, "How did you know that?"

"Look at your posture," he said. My posture at the time was horrible. I had severe rotation in my hips, and my right shoulder was rounded and pulled down and forward (like many golfers). He explained the body's natural and correct posture, and he showed me how severely out of balance I was. From there, Ric described my golf swing tendencies and pinpointed precisely how my poor posture was contributing to my golf swing faults.

I was *shocked*. He had never seen me before, let alone seen me swing a golf club. Yet his diagnosis was absolutely right on. It was like he had a supernatural gift. I was amazed. It was the start of a grand awakening. For the first time, I realized I might be able to end a lifetime of confusion about the golf swing. I might be able to find answers to questions that had been plaguing me since I was a kid.

## THE BEGINNING

My life in golf started back in Santa Barbara, California, where I grew up. At about age seven, I began following my father, Elmer Fredericks, around the golf course. He was a fine player with a beautiful swing and could hit the ball a mile. I eventually got my first set of clubs–Bobby Jones Juniors. There were two woods, four irons, and a putter. Like most kids starting out, I'd take a wide stance and give it a hockey-puck type of motion down the fairway.

When I was nine, my father got me a complete set of First Flight clubs. I couldn't wait for them to arrive. My anticipation was off the charts. Despite

1.1 Roger in the early days.

the fact that they were too long for me, my dad said they would be fine and that soon enough I'd grow into them. I immediately went out to play with them at La Cumbre Country Club, where my parents were members, and I couldn't have hit the ball any worse if I had tried. The new clubs felt terrible. I was demoralized. My dad had left work early and joined me in the middle of the fourth fairway to see how I was doing with the new clubs. He found a very disconsolate son.

He told me to hit a few balls so he could figure out why I was hitting bad shots. He watched for a few minutes, and then he said confidently, "I know exactly what is happening. Because the clubs are longer, you're going to need to take it back longer so you can create more leverage." He told me to take it back low and slow, and swing it back as far as possible—and wait for it at the top. His advice produced a much longer, rhythmic swing. Until then, I had a very short backswing that had worked just fine with my old set, but wasn't well suited for these longer clubs.

## DISCOVERING THE MAGIC AND PASSING IT ON

This actually was my first lesson, and it changed my relationship with golf. It was unbelievable. Every shot I hit was high and long. From that moment, I became compulsive—just by making one little change in my swing. I had discovered the magic that is legendary in golf. That particular day was the beginning of my search for the secrets of the golf swing.

*Most golfers are looking for the magic....*

Most golfers, I came to realize, are looking for this magic in their games. Nearly all golfers spend their lives searching for some swing secrets, or that one little thing that will make a difference. Everybody goes through this, from Joe Hacker to golf's greatest players. I see this all the time in my golf schools, and it never fails to remind me of that day when I first found the magic in the company of my father. I remember it vividly: the flight of the ball, the consistency of my shots, the absolute joy of discovering that one little thing that made such a dramatic difference.

There is purity and innocence to this joy, and it is something I see frequently in my students. We can be incredibly successful as adults and yet, at the same time, we can retain that childlike quality of excitement and zeal about golf.

The game of golf offers a lifetime of discoveries—new swing tips and the overwhelming feeling that we've finally got *it* and *it* won't go away. Even when *it* disappears, as *it* inevitably does, we can get *it* back. Golf, after all, is a quest that never ends. Looking back now, I realize that magic moment with my father was the start of my golf instructional odyssey. It didn't take me long to become one of the greatest golf swing psycho junkies who ever lived. There wasn't a round of golf that I played when I wasn't trying something new or different, and this pattern went on for decades.

## ADDICTED TO GOLF LESSONS

As a junior golfer, I took lessons from several renowned teachers, but ultimately I still played by feel. I received a partial golf scholarship to Arizona State University, which had (and still has) one of the top college golf programs in the country.

In 1972, after college, I turned professional and worked hard on my game in preparation for the PGA qualifying school in the Fall. In June of that year, I suffered a very serious wrist injury, which eventually required two major surgeries. In the first surgery, doctors took bone out of my hip and transplanted it into my wrist. That surgery failed and my wrist got worse. In the next surgery, a year or so later, they literally cut one of my metacarpal bones in half and inserted a prosthetic (which is still there today). This process took more than a year and a half, and I was in a cast much of that time. When I was finally able to resume playing, I noticed a tremendous difference in the way I hit the ball. What I discovered was that my old reliable right-to-left draw, the shot I had hit all my life, was completely gone. It was replaced by a weak push fade that really didn't go anywhere. My accuracy was gone too, along with my confidence.

This confused me terribly. To get back on the right track, I sought golf instruction from anyone and everyone. I took lessons from a legion of teachers. You name them, I probably went to them. If I didn't see them, I read their books or watched their videos, or I picked the brains of people who had seen them. I tried everything imaginable. Even more confusing was that many of these teachers had opposing theories about the golf swing. These theories often conflicted with each other so much that I became entirely confused. When I say I took lessons from them, I don't mean an occasional lesson here or there. I mean I worked at it. I'd sometimes hit 500 balls a day trying to "groove" what they were teaching me.

I also trained with Chinese martial arts teachers to learn and adapt energy transfer and power concepts to the golf swing. More than once, I persuaded a Chinese kung fu master to try to figure out the golf swing. Each one was fascinated and confused by it.

Claude Harmon and Paul Runyan were two of the great instructors whom I saw for several years. Although both were incredibly knowledgeable, their teaching concepts were diametrically opposed to each other. For example, Claude wanted me to play with a weak left-hand grip; Paul wanted a strong left-hand position. Claude advocated a wide stance; Paul liked a narrow stance. Claude told me to keep my hands high at address; Paul wanted them low. Claude wanted me to set my wrists early; Paul wanted me to drag it back. You get the picture? And that was just the address and start of the swing. When it came to the full swing, I was unable to simplify things. Every teacher had a different theory.

I wouldn't be surprised if I drove many of these teachers to their psychiatrist's couch because of the countless questions I asked. While I listened and tried to learn each system, I couldn't help but notice that a high percentage of great players had unorthodox swings. Furthermore, their swings were so distinctive, that seldom did you ever see any two people swing the same way. Just look at the swings of Arnold Palmer, Lee Trevino, Chi Chi Rodriguez, Doug Sanders, Miller Barber, Jim Furyk, and others, and you'll see what I mean.

## *Every teacher had a different theory.*

There were dozens of great players whose golf swings weren't even close to each other. I'd watch very successful players with short swings and long swings, strong grips and weak grips, early wrist sets and one-piece takeaways, cupped wrists and flat wrists, upright swings and flat swings. I would often go to my teachers and say something like, "You know, I was watching Lee Trevino and Gene Littler play the other day, and their swings are completely different. They don't do what you're telling me to do."

Most teachers would tell me those players were "exceptions." That made sense at the time. Yet, it never occurred to me that maybe *I* was an exception. In fact, maybe we're *all* exceptions and are all "uniquely unique."

## CLUELESS ABOUT THE GOLF SWING

This instructional journey lasted nearly 12 years, and my golf game went from pro-tour material to an 8 handicap. The odds were 50-50 if I would break 80. I can honestly say that, after all the different methods and all the different teachers, nobody made me a better golfer. Nobody gave me the "secret" or made me feel confident in my skills. In fact, I got so confused that I was literally lost in a maze from which there was no escape. I barely knew which end of the club to hold. I thought of quitting the game all the time, but I couldn't. I was a psychological mess.

I didn't realize at the time that all my experiences—as a player and especially as a student of all these great teachers—would eventually help me become a better instructor. Everything I went through, all the joy and frustration, would motivate me to understand the complexities of the golf swing. I feel strongly that, to be a good teacher, one has to experience much of this to be able to comprehend what is happening inside the minds and bodies of one's students. Golf is a perplexing mental game, and an excellent instructor has to be a psychologist and a motivator, as well as a master of the golf swing.

## DOCTORS AND FAITH HEALERS

To complicate the situation, my body began to deteriorate as I struggled with my golf game. My left knee was painful all the time. This required two knee surgeries to go along with my two wrist surgeries. Occasionally I suffered from shooting sciatica back pain that would sear down my hip and legs. I didn't know what I was going to do with my life.

The story of my body parallels the story of my golf swing. That is, I went to everybody to fix my knee pain. You name them, I've been to them— orthopedic surgeons, physical therapists, rolfists, chiropractors, deep tissue massage therapists, acupuncturists, acupressurists, martial artists, even a Philippine faith healer (who actually helped). And, just like with my golf swing, nobody or any of their treatments provided a definitive answer.

In fact, with each passing year, my knee got worse and worse until my left patella (kneecap) would literally slide off of its track.

Despite all this, I never gave up the dream of playing on the PGA Tour. I worked very hard on my game with the intent of someday, somehow, making it to the tour. I never gave up that dream—until I played a round of golf one day with Craig Stadler.

## THE CRAIG STADLER DECISION

I was invited to play with Craig Stadler at La Jolla Country Club in San Diego. Craig arrived at the course about one minute before our tee time and didn't hit one warm-up shot. He went straight from the parking lot to the first tee. Despite missing two 20-inch putts, he shot the easiest 65 that I've ever seen. And he didn't seem elated at all. In fact, he seemed like he didn't even care. If that had been me, I would've been celebrating for weeks. Even the good rounds that I had shot seemed like hard work. Never had I shot a round with the ease that he had—and I had been practicing my game for years. Right then, I experienced a moment of clarity. I asked myself, "What in the world am I trying to do? Forget this." And right then I gave up my dream of playing on the PGA Tour. That decision turned out to be a good thing because fate had something else in mind.

## THE MEN WHO CHANGED
## THE DIRECTION OF MY LIFE

When I met Ric McDonald, he had been the head trainer of the San Diego Chargers football team for 19 years. His reputation in the field of physical therapy was legendary. He had recently joined forces with a unique anatomical functionalist named Pete Egoscue (who eventually became Jack Nicklaus' trainer and formed the renowned Egoscue Centers around the world).

Ric and Pete teamed up to start a physical-therapy clinic called T.H.E. (Therapy, Health, and Education) Clinic, in Del Mar, California, and I was lucky enough to become associated with them. As Ric explained to me why all the golf lessons hadn't worked on my swing, he also explained why all the therapy hadn't worked on my knee. The cause of both problems lay in my poor posture, which was related to the muscle imbalances in my body. These muscle imbalances were also the cause of my golf swing mechanics. Ric explained to me precisely how "your body is your golf swing."

## *I had never even thought about the possibility that my body was the cause of my golf swing faults.*

As he was speaking, I was literally in awe and somewhat in a state of shock. I had never even thought about the possibility that *my body* was the cause of my golf swing faults. I had never associated one with the other.

I, like so many people, had always subscribed to the mistaken belief that just by working on swing mechanics I was going to improve my golf swing. Just working on golf swing mechanics however, isn't necessarily going to grow you a new hamstring or increase the length of your hip flexor! This is the very myth that I've been trying to dispel for more than 20 years now. It is the foundation of my entire message today. I had never even thought of that concept before! I distinctly remember telling myself at the time that this guy knew more about the truth of the golf swing than all of the instructors I had seen put together. This truly was the truth about the golf swing.

Finally I asked him, "Can you fix my knee?" He looked me right in the eye and said, "Oh yeah, that's a piece of cake. And by the way, your knee isn't your problem; it's your hips. Your knees don't track directly underneath your hips because of the dominance of your right hip, which has caused your pelvis to rotate to the left. As long as your hips are out of alignment, your knee will never get better." He went on to tell me that, if I followed his advice, I'd not only be pain free in a short amount of time, but I'd be running and jumping. Again I was astounded because every health practitioner had told me that running was bad for my knees.

Ric told me that, for me, this wasn't true. He said that once he loosened the muscles of my legs and hips and began a proper flexibility program, my pelvis would be able to float and my knees would track directly underneath them where they were designed to be. He went on to explain that when my knees were once again tracking directly underneath my hips, I could run 'til my heart's content.

## FIXING MY KNEES

The next week we got together, and he began to put me through a type of therapy that I'd never seen before. He put me in a gravity-relaxation exercise along with some unusual poses and stretches. Within 45 minutes, I could feel the pain leaving my knee. This was magic in itself, and I carefully followed his instructions for the next several months.

Just like he said, in a short amount of time I had no pain. I became dedicated to increasing my flexibility and getting my body back in postural alignment. I started feeling lighter, taller, and more confident. And guess what? As my body began to improve, my golf game began to improve. This, of course, was no coincidence.

At once, I began to learn this philosophy as fast as I could. I couldn't get enough. While I was learning about the body—and specifically my body—I began to learn other things as well:

- Why so many people struggle with their golf games because they don't understand their bodies.

- How the muscles influence the golf swing.

- Why handicaps have scarcely (if at all) come down in 30 years despite the remarkable advances in golf club technology, teaching, and course conditioning.

- How the golf swing is definitely an athletic movement that requires ample flexibility and strength in the key muscle groups.

## THE INFLUENCE OF JACK NICKLAUS

My learning process became more intense after Ric and Pete created their T.H.E. Clinic. In the first few months, Jack Nicklaus came to visit Pete to be treated for his ailing back. When Pete and Jack had completed their session, Jack asked Pete what he could do about his flying right elbow, which is still one of the most famous moves in the history of golf.

Pete explained that Jack's flying right elbow was merely a symptom of his tight rhomboid muscles, which inhibited his shoulder blades and forced his right elbow into a flying position. I watched in wonder as Jack's eyes opened wide. He too became enlightened upon discovering that his swing mechanics were a direct result of his anatomical function. For the first time, he understood why none of the external swing remedies had worked. Jack relayed to us how he had tried virtually everything to keep his elbow closer to his side to remain more connected through his backswing, drills such as a head cover under his armpit and straps around his arms.

I watched in amazement as the greatest player of all time told us his story about his struggle to fix this element of his swing. Finally Jack said something to the effect of, "You know, Pete, this is powerful stuff. I want to help you get the message out there about the importance of anatomical function in the golf swing."

Right then, I knew what I wanted to do with my life and career: I wanted to help get this powerful message out to the golf world—that the golf swing is an athletic movement requiring flexibility and strength in the key muscle groups, that people should address the sport from an anatomical perspective, and that simply practicing golf swing mechanics is usually not enough.

## TEACHING GOLFERS ABOUT THE BODY

Eventually I opened my own golf school. I started spreading the message that the average person doesn't possess enough flexibility to perform a fundamental golf swing. I've been doing this now for more than 20 years, and the world finally seems attentive. It isn't just a few people who are listening. Serious golfers everywhere seem to understand that the modern lifestyle hinders their golf swings. They are savvy enough to know they need help.

I hear people talk all the time about the modern golf swing. I find it so interesting that the modern golf swing is the direct opposite of the modern lifestyle. The modern swing is a very athletic move that requires plenty of flexibility; yet the modern lifestyle reduces our flexibility and tightens our bodies. Since joining forces with Ric McDonald and Pete Egoscue, my entire philosophy has been based on coordinating the development of the body with the mechanics of the golf swing. There is no doubt in my mind that this is the 21st century approach to golf, and I am a very lucky person to be part of this movement.

*My Story*

# *Posture and Balance:*
# We Are All Created Equal

## THE FOUNDATION OF YOUR BODY (AND YOUR GOLF SWING)

People are different. We come in varied shapes, sizes, colors, heights, weights, and tastes. In other words, we are all "uniquely unique" in this world. It is this uniqueness that makes each and every one of us special, and it is this uniqueness that makes life so interesting. Whether it's hobbies, interests, politics, or even our golf swings, it is the differences among people that make our world go 'round. Despite our infinitely varied traits, however, there is one aspect in which all of us are created equal: The musculo skeletal design of the human body is the same for everybody. With the exception of a small number of people who are born with deformities, our bodies are designed with the same blueprint. We are born with this design, and providing that we use and work our bodies properly it will not change. If we guard and protect this design, we will function properly and efficiently in everything we do.

2.1. We were designed to be in motion.

## HUNTERS & GATHERERS

Our bodies were designed by the Creator to be hunters and gatherers. Each muscle and fiber of our being was designed to be in motion from sunrise to sunset, constantly moving. Combined with proper walking, bending, reaching, dragging and so forth, we were designed for activities such as reaping crops, planting seeds, picking fruit, walking up hills and straddling creeks. In other words, we were designed to be in motion.

When our ancestors lived this way in the wild, their constant motion resulted in strong and stable feet; powerful and pliable legs; hips that efficiently synchronized the lower and upper bodies; strong arms, chests, and shoulders; and a head that sat squarely on top of the shoulders. Their lifestyle of hunting and gathering contributed to their overall condition, which was one of strength, flexibility, balance, and perfect posture.

## MODERN CIVILIZATION AND THE DECLINE OF THE HUMAN BODY

Around the start of the 20th century, with the onset of the Industrial Age, the lifestyle and environment of our species took a radical turn. Rather than hunt and gather, or walk and roam like our ancestors did in the wild (*fig* 2.1), the vast majority of the population began a lifestyle that is now altering the integrity of our design. We began to move less and sit down more (*fig* 2.2-2.4). As a result, the human body began to evolve out of its natural design and become out of balance. The perfect symmetry and synchronization of the muscles is now being compromised.

When we sit down, the powerful hip flexor muscles are actually being exercised because they're supporting the upper trunk. As a result, the hip muscles begin to shorten and tighten, and tend to pull the pelvis forward. Not only does this increase the forward (or anterior) tilt of the pelvis, but one side of the pelvis usually becomes more dominant than the other (usually the right side).

Think about the process of driving a car. First we sit down in the seat. Then we engage in the repetitive use of our right foot and leg moving from the accelerator to the brake millions of times over a lifetime. This can dramatically strengthen and tighten the right hip and force it out of balance with the left. Coupled with the excessive anterior tilt of the pelvis, the pelvis will also become rotated due to the dominance of the overuse of one side of the hip. If that's not bad enough, as we sit down more and more in our daily lives, our shoulders begin to lean forward and become rounded. The result is that the majority of people in our culture are out of nature's design.

2.2.

*The modern lifestyle is now altering the integrity of our design.*

2.3.

2.4.

## THE DESIGN

2.5. Face-on view displaying perfect posture.

2.6. Side view.

The proper posture and design of the human body is as follows: From a face-on view (*fig* 2.5), we should see the hip joints over the knees and the knees over the feet, which should point **straight ahead**. The shoulder joints should stack up on top of the hip joints, and the head should be directly in the middle of the body, right on top of the sternum. From the side view, we should see the ear over the shoulder, shoulder over the hip, hip over the knee, and the knee over the ankle (*fig* 2.6). These four joints plus the ear should be in direct vertical alignment with each other. Unfortunately we don't see many people in perfect alignment these days. What we normally see are the three posture types described below.

# POSTURE TYPE 1: THE FORWARD POSITION

2.7. Forward torso tilt.

2.8. Everted feet due to tight and imbalanced hips.

In the forward position, the anterior (front) muscles have shortened pulling the torso forward and out of alignment (*fig* 2.7). In nearly all cases, this condition is caused by the hip muscle shortening due to the sitting down lifestyle, and also due to the many activities that we perform in our daily lives. Because our hips control nearly everything in our posture, they in turn pull the shoulders forward, and consequently tend to round. This forward position is reinforced in our daily lives because we constantly hold our arms out in front of us as we drive our cars, program our computers, and swing golf clubs.

This forward tilt is often accompanied by one side being tighter than the other, creating a rotation of the pelvis. When this happens, a common symptom is eversion of the feet (the Charlie Chaplin look). This phenomenon, called *tibial and femoral torsion*, is a symptom of imbalances in the hips. When you see everted feet (*fig* 2.8), you know that the person's posture is being dictated by muscle imbalances in the hips.

*A short muscle simply doesn't move very well, and a muscle that doesn't move restricts the motion of the golf swing.*

For a functional body and a functional golf swing, we need muscles that elongate or stretch. A short muscle simply doesn't move very well, and a muscle that doesn't move restricts the motion of the golf swing. The secret to reversing this posture is not necessarily stretching out the chest or strengthening the back, but rather relaxing and stretching the hips and strengthening the glutes.

**Impact on the golf swing:** This posture type prevents a golfer from staying down into the shot and restricts hip turns or straightens the legs (*fig* 2.9). In addition, the tightness in the shoulders and pectoralis muscles (pecs) restricts the upper torso from expanding both on the backswing and the forward swing.

2.9. Straightening of the legs due to lower body tightness.

## POSTURE TYPE 2: THE UNDER POSITION

This posture is quite common in the elderly population. The lower body simply fails to support the upper body and, as a result, the hips tend to tilt under. In this weak and unstable position, the shoulders tilt forward to counterbalance the under position of the hips (*fig* 2.10).

Strengthening in the lower body along with increased flexibility is needed to regain proper posture and function.

**Impact on the golf swing:** Due to the lack of strength and muscle tightness in the hips and lower body, the lack of stability will usually result in the golfer losing the brace of their stance (that is, if they even got into a braced address position to begin with [*fig* 2.11-2.12]) and hoisting or lifting the club up while the lower body straightens or the hips flatten out. (See Chapter 7: Flexible Solutions to Inflexible Swing Faults).

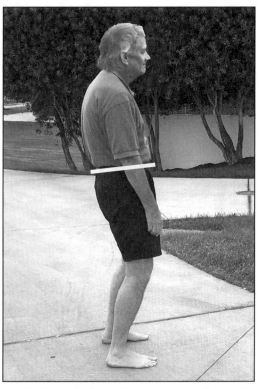

2.10. "Under" hip position due to lack of strength in the lower body.

2.11. Standing "up" and coming out of the spine angle due to a lack of lower body stability.

2.12. A great example of lower body stability allowing a consistent spine angle.

2.13. Notice how the dominant right hip has lowered the right shoulder.

2.14. A rotated torso indicated by dominance in the right hip and shoulder.

## POSTURE TYPE 3: THE ROTATED POSITION

This posture is very common and is present in most people, especially athletes who overuse one side of their bodies (golfers, tennis players, baseball pitchers). Since the overwhelming majority of people are one-side dominant (usually right sided), nearly everybody has some rotation in their torsos. This condition can be detected in golfers by looking at their right shoulders, where you'll usually see a crease in their upper right pec near the armpit. Although the shoulders (usually the right one) are most visible when looking at this posture condition, the hips are really the genesis of the problem. By overusing our right sides so much (such as exercising our legs by moving our flexed foot from the accelerator to the brake millions of times), or by doing the semi lunge squat on the backswing, the hips become overused and too tight. When one side of the pelvis becomes too strong and dominant, the entire body is shifted out of position (*fig* 2.13-2.14).

**Impact on the golf swing:** Rounded and rotated shoulders normally restrict the shoulders from rotating smoothly and effectively throughout the swing. Not only does this restrict shoulder turns, but it is often responsible for the dreaded chicken wing, where we see the arms actually collapse. Although the chicken wing looks like an arm problem, the source of the problem is normally found in the shoulders. In addition, the forward right shoulder is also an indicator that the hips are rotated to the left. Rotated hips and torso invariably encourage people to spin out and not allow a dynamic weight transfer as they shift their weight into the ball of the left foot which generally produce an over the top move (*fig* 2.15).

2.15. Rotated torsos encourage the body to spin out and come over the top.

## A DYSFUNCTIONAL BODY RISKS INJURIES

In all three of these dysfunctional postures, there is one common denominator: The hips have shifted out of position. Once this happens, the entire structure of the body is thrown off. Nearly all joint injuries—back, knees, hips, shoulders, and feet—occur when the hips have changed position.

*A balanced, flexible body is the foundation of a fundamental golf swing.*

Think about it. What's attached to the pelvis? The spine. When the hip shifts, there's going to be friction and pulling with the deep muscles along the spine, leading to back pain, not to mention friction placed on other joints throughout the body.

At the same time, when the hip changes position, the position of the knee changes, creating stress on the knee (usually the medial, or inside of the knee leading to knee pain). When the hip position is altered, the head of the femur, which rests in a cavity of the pelvis called the *ascetabulum*, is suddenly rotated. It begins to grind out the synovial fluid and cartilage in the joint. This creates a bone-on-bone scenario. Hello, hip replacement.

For these reasons, we strive to get the body back in its natural four-socket position, with the shoulders, hips, knees, and ankles all lined up. To get into this position, the pelvis must be restored to its proper position.

## PROPER POSTURE COMES FIRST

It all starts with posture–everybody should strive to attain proper posture. It is more than just standing tall and looking better. One definition of posture is a "state of mind." Posture can provide a sense of confidence and well-being. Everything I do is designed to direct people into a better posture. The better their posture in everyday life, the better their posture in the golf swing, and the better they are going to play. It is all related. A balanced, flexible body is the foundation of a fundamental golf swing.

How do we achieve proper posture? The answer to that can be found in the range of motion combined with reciprocal strength in the muscles.

# Swing Fundamentals

For years, I searched for the answer to the golf swing. I was on a quest and sought out countless teaching pros. In the end, I was struck with the simplicity of what I had learned: Throughout golf history, there have been legions of great players that had unorthodox swings. Whenever I would question an instructor, asking why a particular professional didn't swing as the teacher had recommended, the response would usually be something like "Well, son, they're exceptions, don't worry about them," or "Sure, they swing differently, but they all have good fundamentals." My next question would be "What are good fundamentals?" Or, "What exactly are the fundamentals?"

*Maybe all of us are "exceptions" to some degree.*

As we all know, there are many different theories about the "true" fundamentals of the golf swing. For most of golf's history, the common assessment of these fundamentals has been reasonably clear: Take a good grip, keep your head still, don't look up, keep your left arm straight, return to the address position at impact, and a few others. However, we have learned over the years that the best golfers grip the club in different ways. We have learned that most of them do move their heads, that they do look up, and that the majority of them don't keep the left arm rigid or straight throughout the swing.

---

We have learned that none of them return to the address position at impact because both their hips and shoulders are clearly open when they strike the ball. After years and years, it finally dawned on me that maybe all of us are "exceptions" to some degree. After all, we are all uniquely unique.

Without question, flexibility should be considered golf's foremost fundamental. Without proper range of motion, golfers have to overcome too many obstacles and make too many compensations throughout their swings. In the world according to Roger, flexibility and range of motion are at the base of a consistent golf swing.

But what about the actual swing? What are the fundamentals?

## MY THREE GOLF INSTRUCTION DISCOVERIES

Once I was exposed to high-speed video cameras, I began to understand the golf swing with more clarity. Right away I made three discoveries:

1. It is impossible to give an accurate lesson with the naked eye.

2. There is no one "right way" to swing a golf club.

3. What people think and feel they are doing is seldom what they are actually doing.

As teaching pro Butch Harmon frequently says, "The feel is seldom real." All my life, I have been fascinated by great golf and great golfers. I have tried to be a keen observer of what these players are doing. The key, though, was watching hundreds (if not thousands) of hours of videotape. Pros around San Diego had amassed huge amounts of videotape of top players, and finally it was possible to dispel many of the old myths about the golf swing.

My experience has taught me, and these videotapes confirmed, that there are really only three true fundamentals, all of which apply to the overwhelming majority of great golfers who ever lived.

# FUNDAMENTAL NO. 1:
## Neutral Address Position

3.1. Balanced address position.

The first thing that good players do in their golf swing is address the ball in balance. There are many different definitions of balance. I've heard teachers say that you've got to have the weight on the heels, or drop the right shoulder slightly and tilt the spine to the right. But there are really just two important aspects to determine if a player is in balance in the address position:

1. The weight should be 50-50 on each foot, and the majority of the weight should be on the balls of the feet (*fig* 3.1).

3.2. Balanced address. Notice how the hip joint stacks on top of the ankle.

3.3. Out of Balance. Hip joint outside the ankle, indicating the weight is on the heels.

2. The hip joint should stack directly above the ankle joint (*fig* 3.2). If these two joints aren't aligned, the body is out of balance, pure and simple (*fig* 3.3).

Notice in figure 3.2 that the kneecaps are over the shoelaces, the shoulders are just outside the toes, and the ear is aligned with the spine down to the hip joint. The weight should be 50-50 on each foot, and approximately 60 to 70 percent of the weight should be on the balls of the feet.

Every sport, including golf, is played on the balls of the feet. Biomechanical research has proven this. In the next chapter, we'll explain why. The old notion that the weight should be dominantly on the heels contradicts basic laws of anatomical function. Some golfers have started out on their heels in the address position, but their weight quickly moved to the balls of their feet as they went into their forward press. Nancy Lopez was a great example of this. When she addressed the ball, her weight was on her heels. However, she began her forward press by raising her hands and as she did so, her weight would come off her heels and onto the balls of her feet and into a neutral balanced position. If the weight remains on the heels, it is anatomically impossible to shift the weight effectively with the feet throughout the swing. If the weight is on the heels like many people have advocated, then why is it that skilled players always rise up off of their heels as they swing through the shot?

*...the hip joint **must** stack on top of the ankle joint. If these two joints aren't in line with each other, the body is out of balance, pure and simple.*

However, at this point I want to make an observation. We have been told that the hips and shoulders should always be parallel to the line of flight. (The old railroad tracks image, i.e., the line of the feet, knees, hips and shoulders are the inner rail, and the club head line is the outer rail.) Although this is pretty much true, the reality is that the shoulders will be slightly rotated and aimed to the left of the target line anywhere from 0 to 17 degrees for tour players. Their range for their hips vary from around 2 degrees closed to 6 degrees open. This is due to the fact that we have the right hand below the left hand when we grip the club. This slight extension of the right arm forces the right shoulder to protrude slightly forward, which then has the shoulders aiming *slightly* left. As a person gets older and develops rounded and rotated shoulders, this becomes a problem because the increased rotation of the shoulders will encourage an over-the-top move.

From this neutral position, the golfer should feel light and can move easily into the second fundamental.

# FUNDAMENTAL NO. 2:
## Early Weight Transfer

3.4. The left side of the upper torso shifts the weight immediately to the right side.

Computer analysis shows that the best players shift approximately 70 percent of their weight onto the right foot before the club is even a few feet away from the ball. What's fascinating about this move is that there are so many different ways to do it. Gary Player, Arnold Palmer, and Vijay Singh kick their right knee in and then rebound. Jack Nicklaus has a very slight press with his body into his left side as he cocks his head to the right. After slightly pressing into his left side, Nicklaus then pushes the shaft back with the left shoulder as he moves deep into his right side. Nicklaus has described this as a rebounding off of his left side.

Most players forward press with their hands, or even change pressure in their hands, followed by a rebound. Golfers such as Nick Faldo, Tom Kite, and Curtis Strange bump or squat with their knees and then rebound. Julius Boros bounced the club on the ground before initiating the swing, as did Fuzzy Zoeller and Bruce Summerhays. Whatever the method, the actual backswing starts with a tension release in which the energy slightly pushes into the left side and then is released and flows into the right side.

When I say "flows into the right side," I'm referring to not only the weight moving onto the right foot, but also into the muscles of the right leg and especially the right hip, which goes into a state of contraction, and becomes "loaded." *Loading the right hip properly is arguably the most important aspect of the backswing (fig 3.5).* If the hip is not fully coiled, the upper body inevitably takes control and begins the forward-swing process.

Common examples of unloading the hips are sliding (fig 3.6), overturning (fig 3.7), or elevating the hip by straightening the leg (fig 3.8). Keeping the right hip stable gives you the best shot at having it unwind in proper sequence on the downswing.

3.5. A loaded right hip and braced lower body allows the spine to angle slightly to the right creating the "V".

At the halfway back position (my definition of halfway back is when the left arm is parallel to the ground), we'll see a slight head movement to the right, with the right shoulder deeply turned. We'll also see how the left shoulder has moved away from the left side, which forms the letter "V", or a hypotenuse triangle (*fig* 3.5),

3.6. Hip slide.

3.7. Overturning of hips.

3.8. Elevated hip due to straightening of the leg.

a very common position on a full swing. It is also important to notice how the left shoulder has moved past the left hip and behind the left knee. If we draw a diagonal line across the shoulders at the halfway-back position, we will notice that most good players have turned their shoulders approximately 60 to 70 degrees (*fig 3.9*). Some, such as Vijay Singh and Arnold Palmer, have turned them closer to 90 degrees.

If we compare their shoulder turn at the halfway-back position to where they are at the completion of the backswing (*fig 3.10*), we see that there isn't that much difference. In other words, most of the shoulder turn is accomplished early in the swing.

To make this point even more clearly, the weight that I'm referring to is actually the upper body weight of the left side. In other words, good players turn and shift their upper torsos early and deeply into the backswing against the resistance of the lower body. The more a golfer turns his shoulders *against* the bracing of the legs, the more torque he creates in his body. The bracing

3.9. The majority of the shoulder turn has taken place when the left arm is parallel to the ground.

3.10. Not that much difference in shoulder rotation at the top.

*Secrets of Golf Instruction and Flexibility*

of the legs is absolutely crucial because if there is a caving in of any kind with the lower body, the stretch and torque will be lost. The most common loss of stability in the backswing is usually (1) sliding the hips and too much of a bend in the left knee, (2) elevating the hip due to straightening the right leg, which usually forces the upper torso to lift, and (3) overturning the hips, which forces the weight to go to the outsides of the feet. To better picture this, imagine you're going to shoot a rubber band across the room by placing it around your left forefinger. The forefinger represents your left leg and left hip. The rubber band represents the left shoulder and lats. As you pull the rubber band back with the fingers of your right hand, the more you keep the left finger stable, the more power you'll generate out of the rubber band. If, however, you move the left finger back toward the right-hand fingers, you'll lose all of the energy that you're trying to store up. This stretching is absolutely crucial throughout the golf swing.

From this position at the top of the swing, all the latissimus dorsi (lat) and oblique muscles (stretching from the hips up through the left shoulder) are in a state of what is called *eccentric contraction* (*fig* 3.11). This means that they're being stretched and pulled, and they don't want to stay there. They want to come back to their natural position.

Loading these muscles properly make it possible for the right hip to begin pushing off to start the downswing immediately followed by the left side muscles pulling the torso into the left side. If these muscles aren't loaded properly, the start of the downswing will almost certainly begin with an improper sequencing. This is precisely what we're going to talk about in Fundamental No. 3.

3.11. An illustration of the right side muscles contracting and the left side expanding, all ready to release.

3.12. The lateral/rotational shift of the hips must start the downswing.

## FUNDAMENTAL NO. 3:
### Transition into the Forward Swing: Face-on View

As the lower body is unwinding FIRST during the transition, the left knee will then plant itself on top of the ball of the left foot (*fig* 3.12). This move is the make-or-break point in the entire downswing. When the left knee plants itself on top of the left foot, the dynamic force of the weight shift sends a shock wave up the femur, and in a millisecond, dramatically forces the left hip to begin clearing.

This move is most clearly visible when track-and-field athletes throw a discus or hammer. The more powerfully they land on the front foot and leg, the more effective they are in hurling the object. If the left knee doesn't move back and put weight on the left foot, the golfer does not

3.13. Notice how Sergio Garcia's belt buckle has shifted forward towards the target.

benefit from the power that he has generated and stored up in the back-swing. There is no clear-cut stop at the top of the backswing with all of the body parts. In other words, as the left knee is pulling back, we'll actually see an increased separation between the left and right legs going forward (*fig* 3.13). This increased separation creates more power and consistency into the blow.

The shifting of the lower body actually increases the stretch between the lower body and upper torso. This is the same in all sports, whether it's hitting a baseball or a tennis ball. Watch a baseball batter as he waits for the pitcher to deliver the pitch. Once he picks up the pitch, he'll stride and step into the ball. His left leg begins the separation, but the bat still hasn't swung forward. This is the same sequence as the golf swing and is the most important move in the golf swing motion. At this point, the lower body actually accelerates into the left side, but once it gets there, the hips will brake, and a millisecond after that, the upper trunk moves and brakes, then the arms, then the club. These forces hit the left leg, creating a shock wave up the femur, which then forces the left hip to rotate and create what I call the "two cheek position." It's important to have a stable lower body, because without the solid base in control, the upper body nearly always starts the downswing first, creating a loss of power and direction into the motion.

A moment after the ball is struck, the body and hands release. Somewhere between impact and when the right arm is parallel to the ground on the follow-through, we should see the three fingers of the left-hand glove under the right wrist (*fig* 3.14). This indicates that the club has been released. This position is a result of the centrifugal force created by the turning of the left hip and shoulder, which allow the club to continue to accelerate as the arms and wrists begin the journey upward into the follow-through.

The overwhelming majority of high handicappers either (1) don't release the club and hold on (*fig* 3.15), or (2) prematurely uncock the wrists too early in the downswing. A proper release occurs when the sequencing of the body parts shift onto the left leg and the timing of the arms and hands follows. There has been much controversy on what creates a proper release. Many teachers believe that the release is created by a conscious swinging of the arms and hands; others believe that the release is a natural by-product of the body shifting and rotating properly. I tend to subscribe to the latter mainly because I've asked countless great players with great hand action what they feel with their hands, and to this day, none of them have told me that they're conscious about what their hands are doing through impact. Also when people try to manipulate their hands and arms into the downswing, whether they know it or not, they're often adding pressure and tension to their arms, which slows down the body speed. However I've also seen students who, once they became conscious of releasing the club with their hands, were actually able to also control the sequencing of their arms with their body.

Generally speaking, with good players, I tend to work with their bodies more, and with high handicappers, I try to get them to feel their arms and club more. In any case, the club *must* be released.

3.14. Tiger releasing after impact with the three fingers of the left-hand glove clearly visible under the right wrist.

3.15. Notice the golfers glove above the right arm indicating no release.

3.16. Furyk demonstrating an upright swing plane.

3.17. Garcia with a layed-off shaft.

3.18. Freddie Couples cupped wrist.

3.19. Jack Nicklaus flat wrist.

3.20. Lee Trevino convex wrist.

## Transition into the Forward Swing: Down-the-Line View

Viewing the transition from the down the line view is even more revealing: At the top of the backswing, we see players in a wide variety of positions. We've seen great players with upright-swing planes (*fig* 3.16), layed-off planes (*fig* 3.17), and neutral planes. We've seen great players with cupped wrists like Freddie Couples (*fig* 3.18), flat wrists like Jack Nicklaus (*fig* 3.19), and convex wrists like Lee Trevino (*fig* 3.20). Great players have played from all of these positions.

No matter where a great player is at the top of their backswing, once they initiate the downswing by unwinding their hips, the arms and shaft will drop and come into the ball from a point between their right hip and the right shoulder (*fig* 3.21). The shaft *must* come into the ball from behind the ball, not on top of it. Again, it is the unwinding of the

*Secrets of Golf Instruction and Flexibility*

3.21. The lateral shift of the hips "drops" the shaft under the right shoulder and above the right hip.

hips that creates this position. Unfortunately, the vast majority of high handicappers bring the club into the ball from outside, or above, the right shoulder (*fig* 3.22). This is commonly known as coming over-the-top and is caused by the upper body rather than the lower body, starting the downswing. The over the top move is normally a *symptom* of the right hip not being loaded properly on the backswing, which in turn forces the upper body and arms to get out of proper sequence and start the downswing.

3.22. A classic over-the-top move.

*Swing Fundamentals*

3.23. "Cheek one" and "cheek two" of the fanny are clearly visible in these—and all—great players.

3.24. No cheeks at impact.

## THE "TWO-CHEEK" POSITION

As I mentioned above, *every* tour player arrives at impact in what I call the two-cheek position (*fig* 3.23). From the rear angle, we can see both cheeks of the fanny, the left shoulder aimed slightly to the left, and the right heel off the ground. They are all in this position without exception—some more so than others.

The vast majority of high handicappers arrive at impact with one or no cheeks showing (*fig* 3.24), with little or no shoulder rotation, and no weight off the right foot.

3.25. The shaft reappears at a point above the left hip and left shoulder on a similar path that it traveled on the downswing where the shaft dissected the right shoulder and right hip.

Immediately after impact, the club disappears from view because of the player's body being in the way. When the club reappears, we want to see it under the left shoulder (*fig* 3.25). This is on a similar path that the club was on as it started the downswing.

With the vast majority of high handicappers, the shaft reappears above the left shoulder (*fig* 3.26). If the lower body shifts as it should on the downswing, it will rotate. When it rotates, the club will go to the inside. The club should then finish high but high to the left–fully rotated to the inside, not going down the target line. From here,

3.26. Incorrect: Shaft reappearing too high.

3.27. Shaft "dissecting" head.

3.28. Shaft "dissecting" head.

the club will finish around and behind the golfer's head into what I call the "Steve Martin look." If you recall when Steve Martin began his standup comedy routine, he would walk on stage with the old "arrow-through-the-head" gag. The shaft should dissect your head, just like an arrow going through it (*fig* 3.27-3.28). Just getting into this position cures a lot of swing faults.

In essence, the golf swing motion creates the swing mechanics, not the other way around.

Here is a summary of the three fundamentals:

1. A neutral balanced stance

2. An early weight transfer into the right side

3. A transition of the weight to the left side and into the two-cheek position and finish

Perhaps the biggest problem in golf today, even among some very good players, is that so many players don't transfer their weight onto their left foot on the forward swing. Weight transfer is the shifting of the upper body torso into the right hip and side on the backswing, and the unwinding of the right hip working in unison with the pulling of the left side on the downswing. Incorporated in this process is good balance because, the swing will not be effective without it. I cannot emphasize enough the nucleus of the swing is the body and how well we train it to be flexible and strong will enable it to move with ease.

# DIFFERENT BODY TYPES, SAME FLEXIBILITY

Many people say Tiger Woods has the perfect body type for golf. I don't know about that. Jack Nicklaus isn't built like Woods, and he did pretty well. And Arnold Palmer isn't built like either one of them. Flexibility and strength come in all kinds of packages. One body is not necessarily better than the others when it comes to golf.

The common factors among all good golfers are efficient mobility and stability, which lead to a balanced golf swing. Add power, and what you have is an unbeatable combination as demonstrated by Jamie Sadlowski and John Daly who both demonstrate different body types and superb flexibility (*fig* 3.29-3.30).

3.29. Jamie Sadlowski, 2008 & 2009 Remax World Long Drive Champion.

3.30. John Daly - One of the PGA tour's longest drivers.

# 4

# *What the Muscles Do*
## in the Golf Swing

W̲hat exactly is a golf swing?" The golf swing is a motion performed by the body, which in turn swings the golf club. Since the body is composed of hundreds of muscles, all of which are designed to move and/or stabilize bones and joints, the relationship between the muscles and the golf swing should be obvious: How well the muscles function and interact with each other determines how well the body swings the club. In other words, golf swing mechanics are really symptoms of how the muscles move and interact with one another in this kinetic chain.

In addition, when golfers have strong, flexible, and functional muscles, they are able to perform this motion much easier than golfers with weak and tight muscles. After all, a younger, athletic person, in most cases, has a much easier time hitting a golf ball, tennis ball, or baseball than a senior citizen whose muscles have become tighter and weaker. Let's take a look at the role the muscles play in the body and how they work in the golf swing.

The good news is that no one has to take a course in physical education or anatomy to get an understanding of how the muscles affect the golf swing. However, some basic knowledge is helpful. The Creator designed the muscles of the body to synergistically work with one another. When the muscles function according to their design, we attain perfect posture, and the muscles will also move our joints in a variety of ways that enable us to survive in our environment. These 600 or so muscles all have a specific purpose, or as I like to say, they all have a job to perform.

## HOW THEY WORK

Muscles work in pairs. For example, in our upper arm are the biceps. On the underside of the arms are the triceps. When the biceps contract, the triceps expand and vice versa (*fig* 4.1 and 4.2). This phenomenon is called *reciprocal inhibition*. It is simply the means by which muscles interact with each other.

Another example of how the muscles interact would be lifting a heavy suitcase up to your chest and into the trunk of your car. As you begin the lift, a little muscle called the *supraspinatus* engages and enlists its help to the hand and arm. As the supraspinatus begins to elevate, it cries out for help and the *deltoid* muscle engages and begins to get involved. Finally, as

4.1. A neutral position.

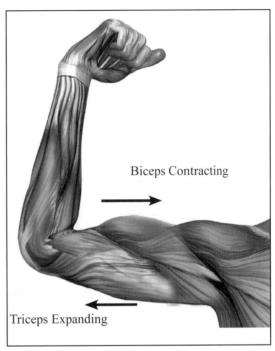

Biceps Contracting

Triceps Expanding

4.2. An example of how the muscles work together.

the suitcase gets higher, the rhomboids and trapezius (traps) help out, and you've got the suitcase up and into the trunk. There is a chain reaction of all of the muscles working together. If one or more of the muscles were weak or dysfunctional, additional stress and pressure would be applied to another muscle. This is the same way the muscles work throughout the golf swing—or any other sport for that matter.

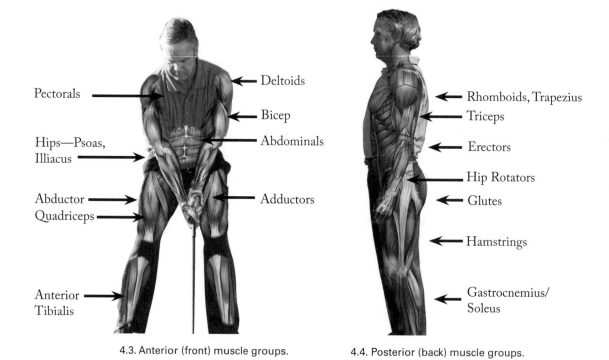

Pectorals

Hips—Psoas, Illiacus

Abductor

Quadriceps

Anterior Tibialis

Deltoids

Bicep

Abdominals

Adductors

Rhomboids, Trapezius

Triceps

Erectors

Hip Rotators

Glutes

Hamstrings

Gastrocnemius/ Soleus

4.3. Anterior (front) muscle groups.

4.4. Posterior (back) muscle groups.

## THE MUSCULATURE OF THE BODY

In the front of our bodies, starting with our lower legs, we have the front of the calves (*anterior tibialis*), the quadriceps, the hip flexors, the abdominals, and the chest (*fig* 4.3). They reciprocate with the backs of the calves (*soleus* and *gastrocnemius*), hamstrings, glutes, lower-back muscles, and the upper-back muscles (rhomboids, trapezii, lats, and so forth) (*fig* 4.4).

Let's take a look at the primary hip flexor (*ilio psoas*), which is by far the most powerful muscle in our body. The ilio psoas plays a vital role because it attaches onto three bones–the femur, pelvis and spine. It also has a major affect on the diaphragm and sympathetic nervous system. When the hip flexors become imbalanced (usually when one side becomes stronger and tighter than the other), every single joint in the body is affected. The maintenance of the ilio psoas is crucial to posture, the golf swing, and all sports activity.

*Secrets of Golf Instruction and Flexibility*

## THE MUSCLES IN THE STANCE

Once we assume the address position, the front (anterior) muscles begin to contract and the back muscles expand (*fig* 4.5). As we tilt forward from our hips, the center of gravity comes outside the body and relocates a few inches in front of our hips. When our muscles work properly during the golf swing, they protect this center of gravity and help us remain balanced. The end result is more solid and consistent contact.

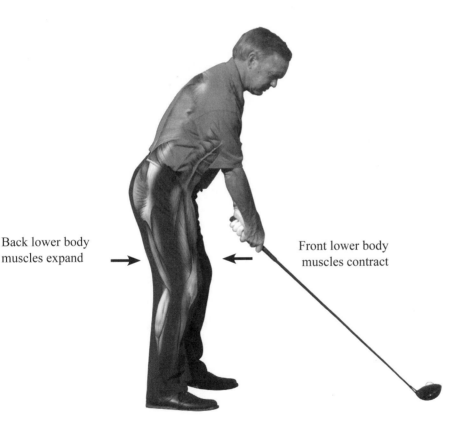

Back lower body muscles expand

Front lower body muscles contract

4.5. Muscles of the lower body dynamically contract and expand in the address position.

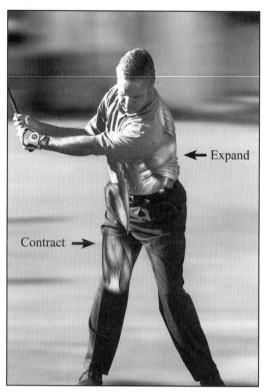

4.6. Lower body muscles on the front of the right leg and hip contract; left side muscles of the upper torso expand.

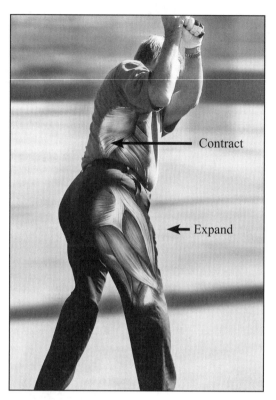

4.7. Muscles on the back of the right leg expand; right side muscles of the upper torso contract.

## THE BACKSWING

Now the action begins. As the left side of the upper torso shifts into the right side, the center of gravity moves slightly to the right. The front lower body muscles, calves, quadriceps (quads), and hip flexors contract (*fig* 4.6) (just as the biceps do in the illustration). As these muscles contract, the muscles in the back of the lower trunk (legs, calves, hamstrings, and glutes) expand (*fig* 4.7). Holding all of this together are the quadriceps and hip flexor working in conjunction with the glutes in stabilizing the lower body. As the front and back of the body are conducting this tug of war, the lower half and upper half of the body are having their own battle. That is, the front of the chest (the pecs) expand

4.8. Chest muscles expand; quadriceps and hip contract.

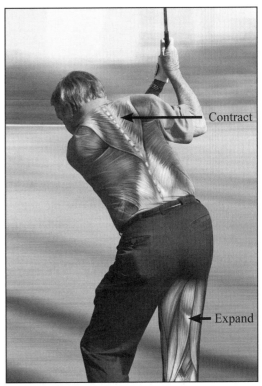

4.9. Back muscles contract; hamstrings expand.

(*fig* 4.8), while the upper muscles of the back (rhomboids and traps) contract (*fig* 4.9). **The front lower body muscles contract while the chest muscles expand**. The lower back muscles of the legs expand, and the upper back muscles (rhomboids and traps) contract.

Tight and shortened muscles on the front side of our chests normally pull the shoulders forward with them, creating rounded shoulders. Rounded shoulders have a damaging effect on the expansion of the chest throughout the golf swing and will definitely produce a restricted shoulder turn and a myriad of other swing faults.

If that's not enough, the right and left sides of the body are also fighting each other. While the right-side muscles contract the left-side muscles expand. In effect, there are three simultaneous battles going on: (1) upper-trunk versus lower-trunk muscles, (2) front versus back muscles, and (3) right side versus left side of the body. In the midst of these battles, all of the muscles are trying to keep the center of gravity in balance.

## THE MOST IMPORTANT MOVE:
### The Transition at the Start of the Downswing

I, like virtually every golf instructor, have been asked "What actually starts the downswing?" The reality is I've asked the same question to many of golf's greatest players, and I've gotten a *lot* of different of answers. No matter what these great players feel, there is definitely a sequence that

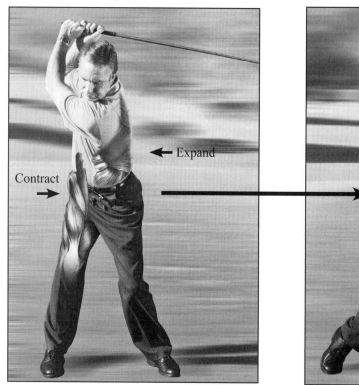

4.10. The right hip and leg muscles push off.

4.11. The left hip and leg muscles pull.

*Secrets of Golf Instruction and Flexibility*

does occur in all of their golf swings. Let's take a look at what physiologically happens from a musculoskeletal point of view:

The powerful hip flexor in the right hip is wound up because it holds all of these "muscle battles" together (*fig* 4.10). It is being loaded, twisted, and contorted, and definitely wants to "get out of there," so it immediately begins to unwind itself. As it pushes off, it works in unison with the left hip and leg, and the weight then begins to transfer over to the left side. In a millisecond, with all this unwinding, the center of gravity moves back toward the front foot. As the weight shifts onto the left side, the muscles of the left leg begin to contract (*fig* 4.11) and do precisely what the right side muscles were doing on the backswing. In other words, as the weight shifts and "crashes" onto the left foot, a shock wave is created that races up the leg and puts pressure on the head of the femur and left hip. These forces then cause the left hip to clear out of the way. This in turn releases the upper trunk. Next the arms are released, followed by the uncocking of the wrists.

This is how it works in the golf swing and in other athletic motions as well. As you can see, an effective golf swing requires quite a lot of muscle interaction in

4.12. Failure to properly load the right hip in the backswing makes it nearly impossible to produce an effective transition into the ball.

the major muscle groups, especially the legs and hips. For example, strong and functional legs provide a great foundation on which the upper body can twist and turn. If, for example, a person has tight hamstrings or weak quads, the hamstrings and quads will not be able to accept the tremendous forces placed on them. The legs will usually straighten up, causing a laying off and then a lifting of the club. The hamstrings are also connected to a little ring around

*This is why **just** working on your golf swing mechanics is not necessarily going to make your body stronger and more flexible.*

the pelvis called the *ischial tuberosity*, so they directly affect the stabilization and rotation of the hips, which affect the center of gravity.

Once stabilization of the legs and hips are lost (*fig* 4.12), the upper body will normally compensate and begin to take over the golf swing motion. In addition to the club being pulled to the inside, the straightening of the leg will normally cause the shoulders to flatten, affecting the hand and club position. This will usually cause an over-the-top move, simply because the lower body has lost control. Many teachers will see this and prescribe a cure for the over-the-top move, when in reality, it was a symptom of the lower body dysfunction (i.e., the straightening of the legs). Another typical example is a person with quadriceps and hips that are too tight or overdeveloped. We see this typically in skiers, bicyclists, marathoners, and bodybuilders. These athletes tend to get out of balance in their legs, a bi-product of the excessive training of their quads and hip flexors. The overtrained, developed muscles become shortened, which then causes them to lose their rotational capacity. This lack of flexibility and rotational capacity generally cause a sliding of the hips out to the right, which results in an upper-body reverse spine angle, and often a chicken wing. This makes it impossible to get the upper body behind the left leg or to get the club properly behind one's shoulders.

Another glaring physical dysfunction is an inflexible torso. (Remember that PGA Tour players have 50 to 100 percent more flexibility in their upper trunks than the average person). When a person with limited mobility in the upper trunk tries to make a full shoulder turn and can't do it, compensations will almost inevitably occur, and can include any or all of the following: lifting, collapsed arms, flattening of the shoulders, and the most dangerous, losing lower body stability. In short, the synchronicity (or kinematic sequence) of the muscle chains are lost. They no longer work together, hence a jerky and choppy motion results. People who have tight *latissimus dorsi* muscles and tight and overdeveloped pecs (bodybuilders), usually have severely bent arms at the top of their backswings. Remember that the pec muscles *must* expand on the backswing. If a person has tight pecs or lats, the shoulders simply can't rotate effectively throughout the swing. The rotation of the trunk creates extension of the arms, and tight trunk muscles usually restrict extension, hence chicken wings.

## GOLFERS ARE ATHLETES

Swinging a golf club is a tremendously energetic, athletic movement. It is no wonder that so many people can't do it effectively. Their bodies do not possess the strength or flexibility in the major muscle groups to perform this highly skilled gymnastic activity. This is why just working on your golf swing mechanics is not necessarily going to make your body stronger and more flexible. This is not enough to allow you to discover or regain a fountain of youth. I advocate a deeper look and new perspective on the golf swing. Rather than work on your swing mechanics alone, first examine how your muscles are affecting your golf swing mechanics. Again, YOUR body is YOUR golf swing. Improving the function of your muscles will obviously improve the function of your golf swing, not necessarily the other way around. For most golfers, this new perspective is a must. But fear not. In the next few chapters, I will show you how you can get your muscles to begin moving as they were designed to move. You can create a freer and more powerful golf swing. You can enhance your enjoyment of the greatest game mankind has ever devised, and it can last a lifetime.

## RESEARCH STUDIES:
## WHY TOURING PROS ARE MORE FLEXIBLE

In the early 1980s, several research studies provided an entirely new perspective on the golf swing. A significant study was conducted by the Biomechanics Laboratory at Centinela Hospital in Inglewood, California. Around the same time, renowned biomechanics pioneer Dr. Gideon Ariel and physical therapists Ric McDonald and Pete Egoscue were conducting their own studies. Among other results, the studies by Centinela Hospital showed that PGA Tour players have an average of 50 to 100 percent more flexibility in their upper trunks than the average person (*fig* 4.13). Incredibly they had even more flexibility on average than NBA basketball players!

4.13. David Duval demonstrating superb upper torso flexibility.

In addition, PGA Tour players had about two-thirds faster hip speed through the shot than the average golfer.

There was some question about why these professional golfers possessed this physical advantage until it was discovered that they had all started the game when they were kids. When you consider how gymnastic the turning of the hips and shoulders are in the golf swing and that they have been performing this motion hundreds of times a day for a lifetime, their superb upper-body flexibility is no mystery.

*Secrets of Golf Instruction and Flexibility*

But how about hip speed? That's simple. Hip speed is a function of how well the leg muscles support and drive the hips. A round of golf is a five- to seven-mile walk, and these pros play and practice nearly every day. They walk, or are on their feet, for much of their lives. Subsequently they end up with incredibly powerful legs, floating hips, and superb upper body flexibility.

Because the average golfer hasn't been out there turning his body and walking as much as these Tour players, and instead has been sitting at a desk or driving a car, it's easy to understand why he ends up with weaker legs, tighter hips, and a tighter trunk. It's no wonder that so many can't adequately perform a fundamental golf swing.

*What the Muscles Do in the Golf Swing*

*Secrets of Golf Instruction and Flexibility*

# 5

# *You've Got to Be Hip*

As we've discussed, the hips play a vital role in the human body. They are the bridge between the lower and upper body. They dictate posture and play a major role in both a person's anatomical function and athletic performance. Even the slightest alteration of the hip joints can affect every other joint in the body. For example, if the pelvis is pulled too far forward due to an overtightening and shortening of the hip muscles (which occurs in the overwhelming majority of people in our culture), the muscles along the lower lumbar spine can be stressed to such an extent that they pull the spine out of position (hello, back pain). In addition to an excessive forward anterior tilt of the pelvis, most people have one side that is usually tighter than the other, which forces the hips to also be rotated.

## *...the misalignment of the hips is responsible for the majority of joint problems....*

This was certainly the case with me back in my younger days, as my hips were not only severely anteriorly tilted, but also severely rotated to the left due to the dominance of my right hip. The severe rotation of my hips to the left, forced my left foot to flare out to the left, creating what's called *tibial and femoral torsion*. With my left hip and left knee rotated outward and turned to the left, a tremendous force was placed on the inside of that knee. This was the cause of my knee pain (and surgeries). Today I realize that I could have had 10 more surgeries that wouldn't have been effective until I straightened out my hips. To summarize, it was the misalignment of my hips which caused my knee problems, not the knee itself.

My experience has taught me that the misalignment of the hips is responsible for the vast majority of joint problems and musculeo-skeletal problems. Only when the hips return to their proper anatomical position can the body's other joints be restored to their correct anatomical position with no undue stress or friction. The misalignment of my hips was also the primary cause of the deterioration of my golf swing and golf game. While my hips were rotated to the left and my right hip and right shoulder were pulled forward, they hindered my ability to turn my right shoulder behind me in the backswing. This also caused my hip and shoulder plane to flatten out and not have enough side bend.

## The golfer's most common problem is tight and imbalanced hips.

With my shoulders and hips on a flat plane, my hips were encouraged to spin out on the forward swing (or, as they say in baseball, "step in the bucket"). The spinout made it nearly impossible to shift my weight onto the forward foot and have my left knee align on top of the left foot. Not only could I not make an efficient weight transfer, but this put a tremendous amount of stress on the left knee and ankle, and in time, began to wear down the ligaments and cartilage in the knee.

A true weight transfer is where the left hip is over the left knee, which is over the left foot. When these joints on the left side stack up at impact, a shock wave is produced from the ground and up the femur, forcing the left hip to clear and create club-head speed and power in the shot. The inability to generate rotational speed around the left hip and leg results in a loss of power, and forces the golfer to compensate in other ways, usually by flipping the hands.

The misalignment of the hips (usually due to the dominance of the right hip, for right-handers) is really the genesis of most swing faults and the No. 1 cause of poor golf shots. Having said that, do you remember what controls bones? The muscles. Restoring function to the muscles restores function to the bones, which restores function to the golf swing motion. The critical nature of the hips in the golf swing cannot be overstated. The function of the right hip is (for right-handers), the single most important factor in the golf swing. All my research and experience gathered over four decades leads me to believe that the golfer's most common problem is tight and imbalanced hips.

Let's take a look at the role the hips play throughout the swing. In a true weight transfer, the right hip engages on the backswing due to the "left side" upper-body weight being shifted upon it. These forces placed upon the hip joint then force the head of the femur to rotate in its socket,

which force the shoulders to turn. Starting down, the unwinding of the right hip (generated by the muscles) forces the hips to shift back to the left. *This is a make-or-break point in the golf swing.* It is here where the result of the shot is determined. In this millisecond, the left hip joint must line right above the left knee, which must stack up over the ball of the left foot. If this doesn't happen, the golfer sacrifices control of the club head.

## STACKING UP

As you can see, the joints of the body are designed to stack up, or align right on top of each other. They are *always* seeking that position. Try jumping off a chair and landing on the floor. Your feet will always come down pointing straight ahead with the knees and hips lined up right above them. In my post-accident swings, my misaligned joints caused not

5.1. Left shoulder, hip, knee and foot perfectly stacked up.

5.2. COG moves slightly out in the address position.

only my injuries but also my golf swing faults. Nearly everything in my teaching is geared to getting the body functioning so that the joints are in proper alignment. At impact on an iron, the left shoulder, hip, knee, and foot should line up (*fig* 5.1). Keep in mind that the left hip will be turned, as will the left shoulder. They are not lined up linearly or vertically, because the left hip has rotated. A driver is somewhat different because we hit up on it, and as a result, we're somewhat more behind the ball than on an iron.

## CENTER-OF-GRAVITY MOVEMENT

The secret to virtually every sport is protecting the center of gravity (COG), in other words, balance. In a balanced body the joints line up properly and, as a result, they function the way they were designed to function. Keeping the body balanced also creates relaxation. This is crucial because relaxation allows the body and mind to function clearly, thus encouraging freedom of movement during athletic motion. Deep within our bodies we have a center. This center is contained in the very middle of our weight, at a point approximately one inch below our navels and one inch in. This is the center of gravity, which controls all of our balanced movements.

Watch a tightrope walker on a high wire: With every centimeter that he moves off balance, the balance pole counters this off-balance movement. It attempts to recenter him. In the golf swing, the golf club reacts much like the balance pole. Research shows that for every centimeter the center of gravity moves during the golf swing, the club head can fluctuate up to 14 inches out of its orbit. In other words, the more the COG moves, the more compensation the golfer needs to make in the swing.

In the golf swing, once we bend from the hips in the address position, the COG moves just outside and in front of the body, and slightly below the navel (*fig* 5.2). Keeping this point quiet is a key factor in

5.3. COG in neutral.

5.4. COG moves slightly to the right.

5.5. COG moves forward to a point where the left hip was in the address position.

the golf swing (from a physics point of view) and directly affects the quality of any golf shot.

I used to study center of gravity movement on the computers designed by Dr. Gideon Ariel, one of the true pioneers of computerized biomechanics. I was fascinated by Edwin Moses, the most acclaimed high-hurdles champion of all time. Dr. Ariel's computers were able to measure Moses' COG as he jumped over the 39-inch-high hurdles. The amazing thing was that his COG hardly fluctuated at all. What really separated Moses from other hurdlers was that they were unable to maintain their COG as consistently as he did, because their COG moved up and down too much. We see this same type of fluctuation in the center of gravity with high handicappers; i.e., the more lifting, sliding, and overall excess movements that they perform, the more the center of gravity is compromised. When the center of gravity is jumping all over the place, energy is lost. Of course, the center of gravity does not stay completely still during the golf swing. Why? We have two pivot points: a right hip and a left hip. For this reason, the golf swing is not a true circle (as was once believed and taught) but more of an elliptical swing arc.

Although our goal is to keep the COG from moving excessively, it must move somewhat to accommodate the shifting of the weight—a little to the right then back a little to the left and then back toward the left heel (*figs* 5.3-5.5). We certainly don't want it to move up and down, although some players do lower the COG slightly as they drop down into a shot. This dropping down into the shot is very common among great players. Tiger Woods and Byron Nelson are great examples of this. However, the players that do drop down into the shot usually stand in a more upright manner in the address position. Golfers who squat or sit low at address have a harder time staying level and usually tend to "stand up" on the backswing and the downswing. It's much better to drop down, than to lift up. When golfers lift up through the shot, they almost invariably lose their lag and their control of the club. This is a power leakage. As the body and COG go up, the club is forced down. We want to store up energy for as long as possible, not prematurely release it.

With the COG in the proper position, the muscles stay contracted during the downswing, keeping the energy locked in and the wrists cocked for as long as possible. This is a result of the forces of gravity and muscle contraction that are being placed on the body, which then rush out through the club.

How do we keep the COG in the proper position throughout the golf swing? The answer is simple: strong and flexible legs and hips (and a strong and flexible upper body doesn't hurt either). Weak and unstable legs and hips will not provide the stability the upper body and arms desperately need to achieve maximum coil and torque, not to mention balance and power.

There is much talk that the lower body isn't that important in the golf swing. Teachers who say this attempt to prove the theory by getting down on their knees and hitting powerful golf shots. The next time you see this, take a look at their hips while they're swinging on their knees. You will see their hips rotate quite powerfully, and their knees are digging into the ground. If these people hit a golf ball while sitting on a table with their feet off the ground, the results would not be the same. Stability with the ground is a paramount fundamental of every active sport.

Let's get back to center of gravity. If the COG rises up on the backswing, you will see a lifting of the club, which takes the lower body muscles out of contraction (*fig* 5.6, 5.7). In other words, the body's muscles will be unloaded in an unproductive move, which increases the demand on the upper torso. The same thing happens when the COG is shifted back on the heels during the backswing. Both scenarios usually result from straightening the right leg, preventing the proper loading of the right hip. On the downswing, we frequently see the COG raising because of the lower body muscles not firing, usually because they were not loaded on the backswing. (After all, you can't unload something that hasn't been loaded). In this case, the muscles have been taken out of contraction (or the flex in their knees), which then impedes a dynamic move into the ball.

Protecting the COG is crucial in the golf swing, and the way to protect it from moving too much is possessing strength and flexibility in the muscle chains of the body. The golf swing is really a lower body game, yet most teachers only teach the upper body movements.

When I was a teenager, I used to go down to UCLA and watch legendary coach John Wooden conduct his practices. Coach Wooden would have Lew Alcindor (later called Kareem Abdul Jabbar) and his entire team perform

5.6. Weight on the heels pulls the COG back with it.

5.7. A raising of the COG due to lack of lower body stability.

footwork drills for the first part of practice. Even though golf doesn't require the jumping and running of basketball, it requires balance and stability to make a consistent golf swing. The drills that I prescribe for my students help promote this balance and stability. Without these two elements at the foundation of the golf swing, a golfer has little chance to improve, and all of the golf instruction that a person receives will normally have minimal effect.

## KINEMATIC SEQUENCING

Over the last several years, more fascinating research and data on the timing and sequencing of the movement of the body parts has been done with 3D motion-capture systems. I believe that 3D motion capture will be the teaching methodology of the future and will eventually replace 2D video cameras, just as 2D video cameras replaced giving lessons with the naked eye. Among other things, 3D technology measures the timing and sequencing of the body parts throughout the swing; 2D cameras simply can't measure these undetectable things. I call 3D technology the "golf swing lie detector test" because everything you need to know is revealed. 3D technology has also shown that virtually all sports that involve hitting or throwing an object have nearly the same kinematic sequencing on the forward motion of the activity.

In an effective golf shot, this is what must happen in the golf swing, starting with the downswing: First the hips begin to unwind and lead the way (as we've described in Chapters 3 and 4). The hips actually begin to shift and rotate before the club reaches the top of the backswing (which is most noticeable in a baseball pitcher's motion). While the hips are unwinding and the club is still going back, an increased stretch occurs between the upper and lower body parts. The "X-factor stretch," as Jim McClean calls it, is increased. In other words, if at the top of the swing the hips have turned 45 degrees, and the shoulders 90 degrees, we have a 2:1 X factor. However, because the hips unwind first (a millisecond before the upper trunk unwinds and the club starts down), there is an actual increase in the X factor. In the case of a 45 degree/90 degree hip and shoulder ration, the unwinding of the hips can actually make it a 40 degree/90 degree ratio. Some power hitters can actually increase it more. Nearly all great players have good kinematic sequencing, and very few (if any) bad players have good sequencing.

In proper sequencing, the hips lead the way followed by the upper trunk, then the arms and then the club (*fig* 5.8). When the forces of

5.8. Notice the explosive hip action of ReMax World Long Drive Champion, Jamie Sadlowski.

the unwinding of the hips shifts over onto the left foot, they then come to an abrupt halt, which catapults the upper trunk, arms, and the club, accelerating them through the shot. The peaking of these segments determines the efficiency of the swing. In kinematic-sequencing graphs, the lines peak above and slightly forward of one another. To picture this, imagine a discus or a javelin thrower hurling his body around and finally planting his front leg right before the throw. An instant after the planting of the foot, a shock wave is sent up the left leg, which forces the hip to clear, which forces the upper trunk to clear, which then allows the arm to swing through hurling the discus. Virtually all sports that involve throwing or hitting something have virtually the same kinematic sequencing.

Another example of kinematic sequencing is the action of cracking a whip. To get a good snap, the lion tamer cocks his wrist back, then snaps it forward, and at the last moment pulls the wrist and forearm back. In other words, the moment he brakes the wrist and begins to pull it back, the snap occurs. If you look at the golf swings of Jim Furyk and Ernie

Els with the naked eye, there is almost nothing remotely similar between them. However, their kinematic sequencing graphs are amazingly similar. We can now look at the sequencing of the graphs of many different players, and without having seen the golfer, we can tell with 100% accuracy who the best ball strikers are! It's that revealing.

The overwhelming majority of high handicappers have poor kinematic sequencing, and in nearly all of them, the hips, upper bodies, arms, and club are always out of sequence. The overwhelming majority of high handicappers start the downswing with the upper body and arms. If golfers don't load their hips effectively on their backswings, their chances of starting down with the pelvis first and then achieving good sequencing is very remote.

This exciting research regarding kinematic sequencing has changed our perspective on what makes a good golf swing. If the body parts are moving in sync, you're going to have much better contact with the ball. And if the muscles are flexible and strong, the sequencing and movement will be harmonious. In summary, the action of the hips will usually tell the story.

# 6

# *Testing Your Flexibility*

This chapter is designed to help you determine how flexible you are, and how your flexibility (or lack of it) is influencing your golf swing mechanics and your posture. We will do this through a series of simple but revealing range-of-motion tests. In all the years that I've administered these tests, I'm always amazed how accurately they explain why a golfer does what he does in his golf swing. When you understand why your failure to perform a certain test effectively is directly related to your golf swing faults, you'll then be on your way to permanent improvement in both your body and your golf swing. I've come to call this the magic moment, because when people begin to understand how the limitations in their bodies affect their golf swings (and they finally know what to do about it), they begin to develop a great deal of enthusiasm and renewed hope in improving their golf swings.

For example, when a person fails in the hamstring test (the runners stretch), we normally see a straightening of the right leg, or an under position with their hips in the setup. I encourage you to be diligent in taking the tests because they will explain what's going on in your body and in your golf swing much more than you'd think. I'll also explain how a lack of range of motion in the tests manifest into some common swing faults. This will help you better understand the role that flexibility plays in the golf swing, and especially, your golf swing. After helping you diagnose your golf swing characteristics, I will suggest some golf swing drills and specific flexibility stretches that will allow you to produce a freer and more functional golf swing. First, though, the tests.

## TEST 1: LAT TEST, PART 1

Let's start with the lat test, which also tests the obliques and the pecs. This two-part test will reveal if you have any restriction in your upper torso and shoulders. The lat muscles (along the back and sides of the torso) along with the obliques and pecs, play an important role in the golf swing, and are crucial in creating trunk rotation and extension for your arms. The lat muscles also stabilize the shoulders, so finding any limitations in their function is a big help in understanding and taking the necessary steps in improving your body and your golf swing. Common symptoms of tight lats and obliques are the collapsing of the arms on the backswing and forward swing (the chicken wing), as well as restrictions in making an efficient shoulder coil. So often people attempt to cure arm and chicken wing problems by putting an elastic band on their elbow joints to keep the left arm straight. In reality, though, the arms are only a symptom of the problem.

The problem usually can be found in the tightness of both sides of the body as well as the pecs. If we see a golfer whose head is tilted forward and his back is rounded, we know this person has an imbalance in the relationship between the pec muscles and the lat muscles, as well as the rhomboids, traps, and levators. In other words, the chest muscles have become shortened and tighter, which in turn pull the chest and shoulders forward. Rounded shoulders invariably restrict the chest from expanding on the backswing, preventing a full shoulder turn. (Such a person almost always has tight and dominant hips as well, contributing to the chest and shoulders being pulled in, but more on that later.)

This test may look simple, but the truth is that most people, especially seniors, have a very hard time doing this. Failing to pass this test almost certainly reveals a restricted shoulder turn in the golf swing. The body will desperately try to compensate in other areas. Many Champions Tour players exhibit a hunched back from the millions of golf swings they have produced over a lifetime, the overuse of the quadriceps and hips from walking thousands of fairway miles, standing on their feet for countless hours on the driving range and putting green, the constant sitting down on airplanes and at dinner tables, plus the swinging of the arms that helps strengthen the anterior muscles of the hips and shoulders.

**Step 1.** Stand about one and one-half feet away from a wall with your knees bent as shown in figure 6.1. Press your lower back, shoulders, and head against the wall. If you can't get your head back to the wall comfortably, or if you do and your jaw line is not horizontal to the ground, you're being restricted by tight lats and pecs. As a result your shoulder turn will be compromised.

6.1. Starting position.    6.2. Ending position.

Place your hands and arms straight out in front of you, making sure that you keep your arms straight at all times (*fig* 6.1).

**Step 2.** Slowly raise your arms up (don't cheat, remember to keep them straight) as far as you can go (*fig* 6.2), and do not let your lower back arch off of the wall.

## Results

If your straight arms can easily go up and touch the wall and your back doesn't come off the wall, you have passed the test and most likely have a functional shoulder turn, one that properly coils and produces a lot of power into the shot. If you can't keep your arms straight and get your hands to touch the wall, and/or if your lower back begins to come off of the wall (which is a compensation), you have restriction in your lats and thoracic area.

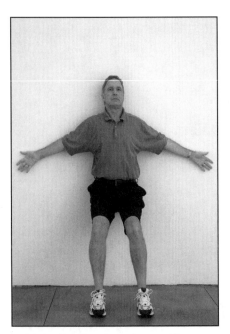

6.3. Lat Test Part 2 starting position.

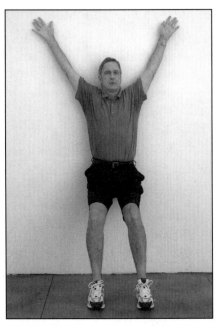

6.4. Lat Test Part 2 ending position.

## TEST 1: LAT TEST, PART 2

**Step 1.** Stand in the same position with your feet approximately one foot off the wall and your lower back and head against the wall. Check to see if your jaw line is level or if your head isn't touching the wall. Now, place your arms flush against the wall in an 8:00 and 4:00 position, with the backs of your hands against the wall (*fig* 6.3).

**Step 2.** Making sure your arms are ram-rod straight, begin sliding your hands and arms up the wall as high as they'll go (*fig* 6.4). Eventually, they're going to begin to bend and/or come off the wall.

## Results

For functional lats, obliques, and pecs, you should be able to get your arms (while straight) at least to the 10:00 and 2:00 position. (Most people just get past 9:00 and 3:00.) It's common for people to "cheat" by bending their arms as they slide up the wall. Make sure that you're diligent in maintaining perfect form during the tests. If you don't give yourself a true test, then you won't get a true assessment.

6.5. Having the arms bent at this position indicates a failed test.

*Secrets of Golf Instruction and Flexibility*

# TEST 2: LOWER HAMSTRING AND CALF TEST

6.6. Starting position.

6.7. Pike up, straighten the legs, and push the heels to floor.

The Downward Dog test will help determine your calf and lower hamstring function. Without stable calves in the golf swing, there will be little chance of having a stable lower body. The calves are actually at the bottom of the posterior muscle chain, which runs from the back of your lower leg up to your neck! Whenever I see a tight calf muscle, I'll normally see a tight back. As strange as it may sound, the first step in straightening out a person's rounded shoulders is to start by loosening up the calves and hamstrings.

**Step 1.** Remove your shoes and socks. Start on the floor on all fours with the hands directly underneath the shoulder joints and the knees directly underneath the hip joints (*fig* 6.6).

**Step 2.** Gently pike up by straightening your legs and pushing your heels to the floor. Keep your knees tight and raise your tailbone as high as you can (*fig* 6.7).

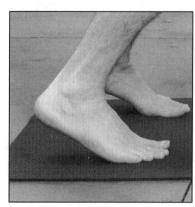

6.8. Severely restricted calves.

6.9. Hamstring test starting position.

6.10. Keep legs straight and flatten the back foot before starting down the chair.

6.11. Hamstring test ending position.

## Results

If you can get your heels to touch or get within half an inch of the ground, you have functional calves and have good stability throughout your swing. If you can only get your heels to within an inch to an inch and a half of the floor, your calves need some work. If your calves are two inches or higher from the floor (*fig* 6.8), you have very tight calves and are severely restricted in your attempt to have a stable lower body in your golf swing. Tight calves work in unison with the hamstrings. If you have tight calves, you probably will have tight hamstrings (not to mention a tight back). In the next test, you will see just how these muscles affect your golf swing mechanics.

## TEST 3: HAMSTRING TEST

The hamstrings are connected to the pelvis and are a major influence in stabilizing the pelvis, as well as contributing to its rotation. Tight hamstrings prevent the pelvis from functioning properly throughout the swing.

**Step 1.** Start by putting your hands on the top of a chair. Then place your right foot forward and bring your left knee flush against the back of your right heel (*fig* 6.9).

**Step 2.** Slowly stand up and straighten both legs and flatten the back left foot (*fig* 6.10).

**Step 3.** Keeping both knees locked at all times, slowly walk your hands down the sides of the chair and see how close to the floor you can get without bending your knees (*fig* 6.11). You will feel some pulling on the back side of your front knee in particular, *but don't bend your knees.* Keep them locked at all times. Most people cheat by bending the front knee in order to get their finger tips closer to the ground. Keeping the knees locked at all times is crucial in determining your hamstring function.

## Results

If you can get your fingertips to touch or get within an inch or two of the ground, your hamstrings are functional and you don't have to worry about lower-body stability in your golf swing.

If you can only get your fingers and hands within 12 to 18 inches of the ground, you have very tight hamstrings. If you can't get your hands and fingertips to within two feet of the ground, you have severely dysfunctional hamstrings and definitely have some problems stabilizing your lower body in your swing, not to mention you'll be prone to back problems. An unstable lower body will certainly produce excessive and compensatory movements in your upper body during the swing. The best way to cure upper body swing faults is to stabilize your lower body.

## COMMON SWING FAULTS CAUSED BY TIGHT HAMSTRINGS
### Flattening of the Pelvis in the Address Position

When a golfer sets up in an address position, the pelvis must be tilted forward toward the ground. Tour players tilt their hips on average anywhere from 7 to 28 degrees. This seemingly simple move is very deceiving and much more difficult than it may appear (*fig* 6.12). The hamstring muscles and the glutes actually must lengthen

6.12. Tight hamstrings will pull the golfer's hips backward, flattening the pelvis and putting the weight on the heels.

to accommodate this tilt, as the hip flexors then contract. In fact, there are a very high percentage of people who simply can't get into a proper address position due to dysfunctions of the hamstrings and glutes. Many simply tuck their hips under, and when told to get their butts up, they straighten their legs and lean too far forward.

If the hamstrings and glutes are tight, they won't allow the golfer to properly bend his hips forward because of the tightness of these muscles. The golfer will tend to sink backwards on his heels, which will also raise the hands and arms at address. From this position, the golfer is doomed even before he begins swinging because the muscles have little or no chance to stabilize the body, thus keeping the golfer out of balance.

## Straightening of the Legs

As the upper body weight shifts onto the right (or dominant) foot and leg, the front quadriceps and hip flexors begin to contract. This forces the hamstrings to expand. However, a tight hamstring (or a weak quadricep)

will not accept the forces being placed on it and the leg will usually straighten (*fig* 6.13). Once the leg straightens, the hip becomes elevated, producing a chain reaction where virtually every part of the body becomes out of sequence. Golf swing mechanics are affected as well, usually resulting in a laying off of the club, followed by a lifting of the club, then an over-the-top move.

A straightening of the right (or dominant) leg usually results in the weight shifting back onto the heels. This move also takes the contraction out of the legs and throws the body out of balance because the center of gravity has been moved rearward. Remember, for every centimeter the COG shifts, the club head can move up to 14 inches out of its proper relationship, or orbit,

6.13. Straightening of the legs is usually due to tight hamstrings and hips.

*Secrets of Golf Instruction and Flexibility*

with the center. With the contraction now taken out of the lower body, the resistance and dynamic tension of the upper body is lost, the shoulder coil becomes slackened, and the hands and arms usually begin flailing away, trying to find their way back home—back to the ball, just like the tightrope walker's pole when he loses his balance on the high wire.

## Flattening of the Shoulders

6.14. Arnold Palmer demonstrating perfect tilt and turn of his shoulders.

6.15. A typical layed-off and flattening of the shoulders.

Because big muscles control little muscles, when the right leg begins to straighten, the direction of the forces are pulled inside and the shaft is sucked along with it. The club will then "lay off" and swing on a flatter swing plane. Again, much like the tightrope walker, the body, always seeking balance, will recognize this and begin to lift the club (the pole) in an effort to regain balance. The club then begins its journey outside and over the top, a move that all golfers try to avoid.

The shoulders in a functional golf swing should maintain their 90-degree relationship with the spine angle that was established in the address position. In other words, at the top of the swing, the clavicles should be pointing down and perpendicular to the spine, which is usually set at about a 40- to 45-degree angle.

Another way to picture this is the shoulders at the top of the backswing should be parallel to the shaft angle established at address (*fig* 6.14). However, when the right leg straightens due to tight hamstrings, the pelvis will usually overrotate, which in turn affects the spine and shoulders. The shoulders are now drawn into the act and they too begin to flatten (*fig* 6.15), coming out of the spine angle created at address. Since the shoulders control the arms, the arms lose control and in turn, the wrists will not hinge in the proper sequence.

Because the hamstrings also have a major influence on the pelvis, this tightening usually restricts the freedom of the hips in not only the backswing but also the forward swing. Without pelvic rotation, the golfer cannot effectively shift his weight with the lower body and therefore will not be able to maximize club-head speed.

This usually results in "no cheeks" at impact. Because the hamstrings are tight, this results in an early straightening of the left leg as the golfer swings into the shot (just the reverse of the backswing). It is okay for the left leg to straighten, but it has to come *after* the weight has already shifted to the left foot. A premature straightening of the left leg forces the hips and shoulders to brake too soon which usually produces an out-to-in swing path coming into the ball. As a result, the ball will start out to the left.

## Arms
Because tight hamstrings tend to straighten the legs and produce a premature braking action, this also causes the hips to jam. Once the hips jam and stop rotating, the centrifugal force generated by the body is interrupted and the arms lose their extension, resulting in the infamous chicken wing finish.

This dreaded position is the result of the collision between the body and the arms. The straightening of the leg is often the reason for the premature uncocking of the wrists. So, tight calves and hamstrings play a big role in every action in the upper body and arms. Even a slight increase in the range of motion in the calves and hamstrings makes a huge difference in producing a functional golf swing.

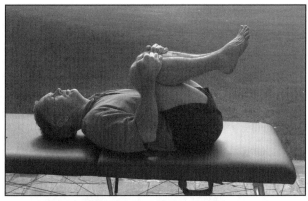

6.16. Knees back toward shoulders as far as possible.

## TEST 4: HIP FLEXOR TEST (THE THOMAS TEST)

This test will tell a lot about the functioning of your hips. How the hips function in the golf swing (and in every sport for that matter) is paramount. Even the slightest movement of the hips will affect every joint in the body. If you are overweight, this test won't be accurate; proceed to the alternate test that follows.

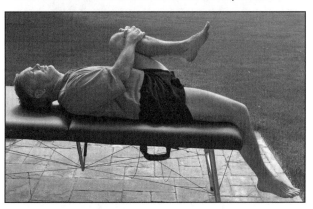

6.17. Pull the left knee toward the left shoulder and *slowly* lower the right leg down towards the table.

**Step 1.** Sit on the edge of a massage table (or the top of a stairwell, a counter top, or table). Make sure that the middle of your thigh is on the edge of the table.

**Step 2.** Simultaneously take hold of each knee just below the kneecap with your hands. Roll all the way back and allow your head to rest on the table.

**Step 3.** With your head on the table, pull your knees back as far as you can toward your shoulders (*fig* 6.16).

**Step 4.** Take your right hand off the right knee and put it on the left knee, assisting the left hand. Using both hands, keep pulling the left knee even more, so that it draws even closer to your left shoulder (*fig* 6.17). Slowly relax the right

6.18. Functional hip.

6.19. Tight hip.

leg and let it come back down toward the table. Don't force the right leg down; let it come down very s-l-o-w-l-y.

## Results

If your right hip is functional, the entire right leg will settle directly onto the table (*fig* 6.18). This is rare, however. If the leg doesn't return flat on the table but instead produces a gap between the leg and the table (*fig* 6.19), you definitely have a tight right hip. Be sure to repeat on the other side and compare. Excess *baby fat* around your midsection won't allow an accurate test, so if that's the case, take the alternate test that follows.

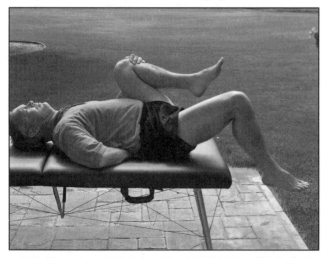

6.20. Alternate test. Note how the right thigh has lifted off of the table and that the right lower leg is not pointing straight down, indicating a tight hip and quad.

## ALTERNATE TEST

Follow step 1 of the test. Then, with your left hand, pull back your left knee. Place your right hand under the small

*Secrets of Golf Instruction and Flexibility*

of your back (*fig 6.20*). When you pull your left knee back, check to see if your right leg rises off the table. If it does, you have a tight right hip. If it severely comes off the table, you have a very tight right hip. Also, check to see if the right calf (which was hanging off the table) has shifted. If it has elevated upward, it is also an indication that you have an overly tight right quadriceps (quads). If this is the case, you definitely have tight quads and hip flexors. Tight hips hinder every aspect of your golf swing. Your hips will have a difficult time blending the proper amount of rotation and stability throughout your golf swing, and often "compensate for compensations."

## Effects on the Golf Swing

A tight right hip is the No. 1 problem in golf, for it affects *everything*. People with overdeveloped quads, such as bicyclists, marathon runners, skiers, and bodybuilders, tend to lose their rotational capacity due to the overdevelopment of their strong quads and hips. Overstrengthening a muscle shortens it. When it is shortened, it doesn't move efficiently. This in turn reduces a muscle's rotational capacity.

Let's look at golfers with this condition. When they begin to shift their upper-body weight in the backswing, the tight hips usually don't allow them to achieve a natural rotation. As a result, the hips tend to slide out to the right. This move is usually catastrophic and leads to many other faults, such as moving the weight to the outside of the right foot, forcing the upper body into a reverse mode, flattening the shoulders, and producing a flying right elbow. Why the elbow? Remember the sequence of the body: legs control hips, hips control shoulders, shoulders control arms, arms control hands. If the hips are tight, the odds are that the chest will be tight, and if the chest is tight, it won't expand, forcing the arms to collapse.

In the backswing, when the hips begin to turn, the shoulders begin to turn. They turn on the axis of the spine, which is tilted forward about 35 to 45 degrees. The left shoulder will tilt down approximately six to eight inches, and the right shoulder will rise up about the same amount. What happens when the right shoulder rises? The right arm has no choice but to fold,

---

*Testing Your Flexibility*

which in turn folds the wrists, which cocks the club. When the right hip slides, this stops the proper rotation of the hips. It also impedes the rotation of the shoulders, which in turn prevents the right arm from folding. In an attempt to gain freedom, the right arm then begins to fly and lift up and outward from its intended plane.

One of the biggest swing faults is the blocking of the hips at impact—no two-cheek position. The proper rotation of the hips on the forward swing is just not there. A sliding hip usually creates a reverse tilt of the upper body, so the upper body wants to get back in position by moving first on the downswing. The upper body and especially the left shoulder must stay *behind* the left leg at all times until the majority of the weight shifts onto the left foot. The lower body must initiate the downswing, followed by the trunk, arms, hands, and club head.

Tight hips are responsible for other swing faults, namely too much hip turn and, at times, too much shoulder turn. Too much hip and shoulder turn on the backswing will usually lead to not enough hip and shoulder turn on the forward swing. In other words, we want to create a maximum amount of separation or torque in the midsection of our body. This is the result of a stable lower body and a fully coiled upper body.

If a person's hips are too tight, there will usually not be adequate torque (X factor). Because the body knows it can't create separation between the lower trunk and the upper trunk, the hips *and* shoulders will overturn. A 45-degree hip turn and a 90-degree shoulder turn will produce a 2:1 ratio. If a golfer turns his hips 70 degrees and his shoulders 120 degrees, they have decreased the amount of torque and coil they are trying to achieve. Invariably, an overturn of both the hips and shoulders result in a straightening of the right leg. By now, we all know what that produces.

## TEST 5: SHOULDER TURN TEST

Everybody in golf wants a bigger shoulder turn, and for good reason. Coiling the shoulders properly against the resistance of the lower body pays huge dividends. It produces power and consistency, which mean longer and straighter drives, and more greens in regulation. Getting all that body mass behind the ball and then releasing it is imperative in the golf swing. The problem, however, is that very few people are capable of making the big turn that they see the Tour players make so effortlessly. The average golfer is incapable of making a true 90-degree shoulder turn. As a result, he usually gets in a world of trouble when trying to do so. This test shows you just how much of a turn you can make.

6.21. Shoulders in line with extended left leg indicating functional upper torso turn.

**Step 1.** Start by sitting down with your legs extended. Sitting upright, bring your right foot over your left leg, just outside the knee. If you can't get your right foot up as high, or higher, than your knee, place it further down your leg closer to your left foot. If you can't get your foot above your knee, it's not a big deal. Just make sure you keep your foot flat on the ground.

**Step 2.** Place your right hand directly behind you so that your fingers are pointing directly away from you, ideally in the midline of your body. Keep your left arm straight and place it across your chest so that it is pressing onto your right thigh. Turn your head as far behind you as you can, theoretically looking over your right shoulder (*fig* 6.21).

## Results

Now check out the position of your shoulders. If they are not in line with your extended left leg, you lack the necessary flexibility to make a true 90-degree shoulder turn (*fig* 6.22). In fact, looking at the angle of your shoulders in relation to your extended left leg will almost invariably give you the number of degrees that you can turn your shoulders. In other words,

---

*Testing Your Flexibility*

6.22. Example of a failed shoulder turn test. Student is unable to get the shoulders in line with the extended leg.

if your shoulders are approximately 75 degrees in line with your leg, you probably can make a 75-degree shoulder turn (without cheating).

What do I mean by cheating? The following test will you give you a clear understanding of the relationship between the shoulders and hips and how they synchronize with each other.

## ALTERNATE SHOULDER TURN TEST

**Step 1.** Lie on the ground in a fetal position with your thighs angled 90 degrees from your torso and your lower legs angled 90 degrees from your thighs (*fig* 6.23). Place your arms directly out in front of you with your hands in prayer.

**Step 2.** Keeping your knees together (and without letting your top knee slide off), swing your top hand and arm all the way back over to the floor. Let your head come back so that you're looking straight up at the ceiling (*fig* 6.24). (*Again, don't let the top knee leave its original position*). Most people can't get their top arm on the ground. How far your arm is off the ground will tell you just how far you can turn your shoulders.

If you can't get your arm and shoulder on the ground, what's the only way that you can? Let go of your legs and you'll see. As you release your top knee and leg, you'll notice that your arm and shoulder hit the ground. Is this a true shoulder turn? Of course not. By letting go of your leg, you've lost all the torque and coil that you've stored up. In other words, you've lost your X factor. This is a clear example of what the body does in the golf swing when it is physically unable to perform a movement in the golf swing. Other parts of the body help out and compensate. The body then

*Secrets of Golf Instruction and Flexibility*

6.23. Lower legs angled 90 degrees from thighs and thighs angled 90 degrees from torso.

6.24. Top hand and arm swung back with head turned back.

begins to compensate for compensations, and the entire kinetic chain of dominoes becomes chaos.

## TEST 6: SITTING WALL TEST

I love this stretch, although most people hate it, including Arnold Palmer (at least he used to). When I put Mr. Palmer into this stretch the first day I worked with him, I thought it might be the end of our new relationship. He wasn't happy sitting against that wall down at Bay Hill. Many of you won't be happy either (at first).

The good news is that by diligently practicing this and the rest of the stretches in my program (in chapter 11), you will come to look forward to this pose—just like Arnold Palmer does. More good news: The easier this pose gets, the better your golf swing will function, *guaranteed!* This not only stretches out the muscles in the lower body (specifically, calves, hamstrings, and glutes), but also coordinates all of the muscles along the entire posterior muscle chain. In other words, it also stretches all the muscles up the back as well. Believe it or not, your body wants to be in this position and, in time, will do it easily.

**Step 1.** Sit as close to a wall as you possibly can, ideally with your tail-bone touching the wall. Keep your legs straight with your knees pressed together, and pressing into the floor. If your knees don't quite make it, don't worry about it. Arch your feet straight back toward you (*fig* 6.25).

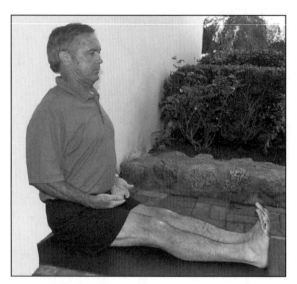

6.25. Sitting wall test.

**Step 2.** Do a shoulder shrug using your upper body, and try to get your shoulder blades flush against the wall. Place the back of your head against the wall with your chin down toward your sternum. Your jaw should be parallel to the floor. This position is your goal. If you can't get into it, that's okay for now. If you can't keep your legs straight on the floor, your knees together, or your chin down and your shoulders back, don't force it. Just be aware of where your body is.

## Results

If you can't keep your legs down or in a straight line, you have hamstring and lower body dysfunction. If you can't keep your back against the wall while your jaw line is level, then you have tightness in your upper chest and shoulders (*fig* 6.26). As far as your golf swing goes, since your chest is too tight and won't expand, you will have a hard time getting your back to the target. How well you perform this test will demonstrate how well your upper trunk and your lower trunk work with one

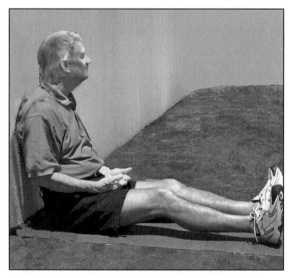

6.26. Failed Sitting Wall test.

another. If you can't do this test very well, you won't be able to maintain lower body stability in your swing. When you are able to do the Sitting Wall comfortably, you will be amazed at how this will positively affect your golf swing. Because all the muscle chains will be in sync, you will be able to maintain both stability and your spine angle. This pose will probably test you, but it will also tell you a lot about where you are (or aren't) and where you need to go.

## SUMMARY

Although I've isolated these tests and pointed out how your performance in them influences your golf swing mechanics, the body has a magnificent way of compensating for compensations. In other words, you may fail in some of the tests and not have the swing faults that have been described here. This means that some muscles in other parts of the body have picked up the slack and taken over for many of your dysfunctional muscles.

The more range of motion and function that your muscles have, the more efficient your movement and your golf swing will be. This is how the Creator designed your muscles to interact with one another. Once your muscles begin to achieve greater range of motion, this smooth-working kinetic chain will produce a freer and more powerful golf swing.

# Flexible Solutions to Inflexible Swing Faults

As far as I know, nobody in history has achieved a perfect golf swing. Everyone has some fault in their golf swing that is unique to them, whether it's Nicklaus's flying right elbow, Tiger's dip into the ball, or Sam Snead's slight inside-and-over move. Even Ernie Els's magnificent swing sometimes has a little hitch at the top of his swing. Everybody has something in their swing that they fight for a lifetime.

The big question is are these *faults* just *habits*, or are they symptoms of that individual's anatomical function or dysfunction? I've learned that, most of the time, it is the latter. In other words, *your* body is *your* golf swing, and to cure these faults one must usually start with changing one's body and anatomical function.

Golfers have taken millions of lessons, which have included endless theories and philosophies on how to fix and cure swing faults. Golfers are constantly thinking of how *this* little adjustment or *that* new move will magically cure their swing faults and create a more effective swing. This has gone on for hundreds of years and probably will go on for eternity. Very seldom do quick fixes really fix a golf swing for an extended period. Most players will try another tip as soon as the current one stops working. There really is no answer. Or is there?

The very premise of this book is to help people realize that for hundreds of years there has been a myth in the game of golf: **The myth is just by working on golf swing mechanics or by taking lessons a golfer will be able to fix or correct swing faults**. But it doesn't always work that way.

The notion that "practice makes perfect," or even "perfect practice makes perfect," is not necessarily true, especially as golfers reach senior status. Most seniors should focus more on improving their flexibility and less on perfecting their golf swings. Again, *your* body is *your* golf swing.

*...in order to make an effective change in a person's golf swing, the functioning of that person's body has to be changed.*

It is widely believed that hard work, dedication, and persistence are the keys to great golf, yet most golfers do not automatically improve simply by taking lessons or working diligently on their swings. Why is it so hard for most people to correct the faults or tendencies in their golf swings?

Yes, golfers sometimes fall into habits that are fixed by rudimentary instruction. However, in most cases, in order to make an effective change in a person's golf swing, the functioning of that person's body has to be changed.

As an example, an elderly golfer (72 to 75 years old) came to see me for a golf lesson. Before we got started, I asked him about his goals and expectations from this lesson. (There are always two stock answers: [1] to be more consistent; and, [2] to hit the ball farther, or both). This gentleman replied that his main goal was to gain more distance. I asked him if he expected to hit the ball as far as Tiger Woods when the lesson was over. As I expected, he looked at me quizzically and replied, "Are you some sort of comedian? Of course not. I could never hit the ball as far as Tiger Woods." I said, "Tell me exactly why you don't think you ever could." The man replied, "Because he's nearly three times younger than I am!" I then responded, "What exactly does being younger have to do with it?" I could see the man's frustration rising, but he did give me the right answer. He simply said this: "Hell, he's much stronger than me, he's much more flexible than me, he has more vitality, and his nerves are better than mine!"

This was exactly what I was trying to get him to say. I then said, "Oh, so if that's the case, wouldn't you agree that if we got you stronger, more flexible, with more energy and vitality, you'd probably gain the distance that you're looking for?" With a newfound enlightenment, the man looked at me and said, "Of course, but at my age, is it even possible to regain more strength and flexibility?" "Absolutely," I said. I told him he could get it back, but not by *just* taking a golf lesson. By doing the proper stretches, in the correct way, and by following a regular fitness program, he definitely could regain much of the strength and flexibility he had lost. Furthermore, an increased range of motion, along with more power generated from his body would automatically result in more club head speed and more power in his shots.

To most golfers this is obvious. The truth is that most people fail to look at their golf swings from this perspective and fail to recognize that their body is indeed their swing. Instead, they usually have the misconception that finding the right swing tip will provide the ultimate answer to their golf swing troubles. Always remember that just working on the new tour move isn't going to grow a new hip flexor or hamstring! To repeat, your swing faults will more than likely remain, especially if you're getting older, unless you change your anatomical function and especially your range of motion. So many older people tell me, "I'm too old to exercise and do all that stuff." To them I say, "You're too old not to."

In this chapter we're going to take a look at several of golf's most common swing faults and explain how these particular faults are usually symptoms of a lack of flexibility and strength in certain muscle groups of the body. Each swing fault will have a menu of stretches, exercises, and swing drills that will help remove those swing faults once and for all. By combining the stretches (in Chapter 11) and the drills (in Chapter 8), you should be able to make some permanent changes in your body. Subsequently, you should be able to make a freer and more powerful golf swing.

Do these exercises for 7 to 10 days, and then the normal stretching protocols in Chapter 10, or, simply combine them with your normal daily stretching protocols.

## FAULT NO. 1: POOR ADDRESS & TAKEAWAY PROBLEMS

A good golf swing must begin in balance. If a golfer is out of balance in the setup, virtually everything that happens from that point on will be a compensation, and often, compensations for compensations will follow. Much like the domino theory, how the first domino falls will influence all of the other dominos in the chain.

I've learned through a lifetime of golf that getting into a balanced address position is often taken for granted, by not only students, but even some instructors. People who have tight quads, hips, and hamstrings not only have a difficult time assuming the position, but in many cases, physically can't do it effectively. I've also learned that there have been many different definitions of balance, but the truth is that physiologically there are only a few key points. They are as follows:

1. The weight must be 50-50 on each foot with the majority of the weight being on the balls of the feet—just under the shoelaces.

2. The hip joints must align directly on top of the ankle joints.

We also like to see the knees over the shoelaces, and the shoulder joints just outside the toes. From there, the arms will be allowed to hang comfortably downward. If these two factors aren't met, the golfer is, pure and simple, out of balance.

7.1. Weight on heels. Note the hip joint is outside the ankle.

*Secrets of Golf Instruction and Flexibility*

For many centuries most golf instruction taught us to sit back on the heels, and the majority of golfers do tend to sit back on their heels which, in turn, rounds their shoulders. But, if a golfer keeps the weight on his heels, it is impossible for him to shift his weight effectively throughout the swing. When the weight is on the heels (*fig* 7.1), the back will tend to round, which will influence a flat shoulder plane, coupled with a lifting of the arms as the golfer goes into his backswing.

## TAKEAWAY PROBLEMS

Most poor takeaway problems nearly always come from a poor address position, which, as mentioned above, is usually caused by tight quads, hamstrings, and hips, not to mention restrictions in the upper torso. We want the weight to move smoothly and effortlessly into the right foot and leg so as to load the hip. The best way to do this is to have the weight distributed evenly before the initial takeaway.

If, however, a golfer begins to shift into the right foot, and the aforementioned muscles are tight or weak, the lower body muscles will not accept the forces placed upon them and will tend to bail out, resulting in a straightening of the leg and an elevation of the hip (*fig* 7.2). As the leg straightens, the shoulders also follow suit and begin to flatten, which will usually pull the shaft to the inside. Now too inside, and the club feeling heavy, the golfer will instinctively lift the shaft up and begin the path to the infamous over-the-top move. Imagine the tight rope walker on the high wire. Every centimeter he moves out of balance, the balance pole will instinctively counterbalance the force in an effort to regain balance and equilibrium. The body and the shaft react in precisely the same way.

7.2. Straightening of the right leg.

---

The best way to get set up properly and take the club away smoothly is to have a balanced set of muscles throughout your torso. After all, how can you take a person with poor posture and suddenly expect him to achieve good posture in the setup?

The the most common golf swing faults in the takeaway that I see are:

1. Straightening of the right leg

2. Improper loading of the hips (either overturning, or underturning)

3. Yanking the club to the inside

4. Flattening the shoulders

5. Reversing

6. Breaking the wrists too early (this often creating a sliding of the hips)

The following drills and stretches will help you achieve a solid address position and help you make a proper takeaway.

## Golf Swing Drills

1. CLOSE-THE-EYES
(D1, page 109)

2. FOAM ROLLER
(D3, page 112)

3. PUSH-AWAY
(D5, page 117)

4. BASEBALL
(D8, page 120)

**Stretches**

1. COUNTER
(S23, page 179)

2. DOWNWARD
DOG
(S1, page 165)

3. RUNNERS
(S3, page 166)

4. EXTENDED
LATERAL
(S28, page 182)

5. SPREAD-FOOT
FORWARD BEND
(S2, page 165)

6. PSOAS
(S15, page 173)

7. HIP-THIGH
EXTENSIONS
(S19, page 176)

8. LATERAL BALL
ROLLS
(S42, page 193)

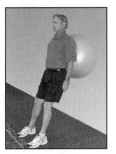

9. WALL SQUATS
(S46, page 197)

*Flexible Solutions to Inflexible Swing Faults*

## FAULT NO. 2: HIP SLIDING (AND NO CHEEKS)

Another dangerous fault is the sliding of the hips, especially on the back-swing. This swing fault is normally a result of tight hip flexors and tight quads and is especially common with bicyclists, marathoners, skiers, and bodybuilders. These athletes tend to overtrain and overdevelop their legs and hips in these types of activities. When a muscle gets overstrengthened, it tends to shorten and tighten. When a muscle gets shortened, it simply won't move as well. From my perspective, a muscle that doesn't move is a weak muscle. We want a muscle that moves easily and fluidly throughout its entire motion.

Tight quads and hip flexors make it difficult for the hip muscles to rotate properly. As a result, when the weight begins to shift into the hips, the muscles do not have the capacity to rotate properly, and they begin to slide out to the right.

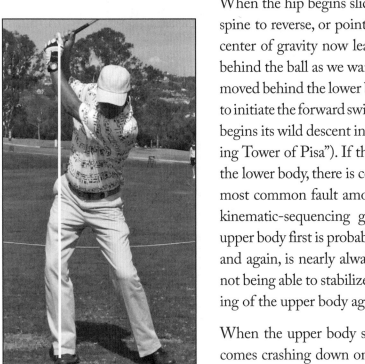

When the hip begins sliding, this usually forces the upper spine to reverse, or point back to the target (*fig* 7.3). The center of gravity now leans back toward the left and not behind the ball as we want. Because the upper body hasn't moved behind the lower body (and allowed the lower body to initiate the forward swing), the upper body takes over and begins its wild descent into the ball (what I call the "Leaning Tower of Pisa"). If the upper body starts down before the lower body, there is certainly trouble ahead. This is the most common fault among higher handicaps seen in the kinematic-sequencing graphs. Starting down with the upper body first is probably *the* most common fault in golf, and again, is nearly always a symptom of the lower body not being able to stabilize and allow the twisting and turning of the upper body against it.

When the upper body starts down first, the club usually comes crashing down on a path that is over the shoulder and down into the ball at a steep angle, aka "over the top."

7.3. Classic hip slide.

*Secrets of Golf Instruction and Flexibility*

When the lower body initiates the downward swing, the arms and club drop down at a shallow angle coming in from behind the ball, not on top of it. The answer to this swing fault is to simply stretch and relax the legs and hips (and often to strengthen the glutes), which allow the lower body to stabilize and create a dynamic stretch between the upper and lower torsos. Use the following drills and stretches to regain proper hip rotation and function.

**Golf Swing Drill**

1. ELBOW-TO-WALL
(D6, page 118)

**Stretches**

1. STANDING DROP-OFF
(S13, page 172)

2. ACTIVE GROIN
(S14, page 172)

3. SUPINE LEG CHAIN
(S8, page 168)

4. PSOAS
(S15, page 173)

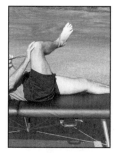

5. HIP ROTATORS
(S21, page 178)

6. HIP CROSSOVERS
(S20, page 177)

7. PRETZEL
(S32, page 185)

8. SOLO SITTING WALL
(S18, page 175)

9. SUPINE GROIN
(S49, page 199)

## FAULT NO. 3: RESTRICTED SHOULDER TURN

Everybody wants to make a bigger shoulder turn and understandably so. The problem is that if you don't have flexible hips or a flexible upper torso, it's not going to happen (*fig* 7.4). However, by maintaining a solid brace with your lower body, you'll automatically create a bigger X factor. For the average player with restricted flexibility, a smaller hip turn on the backswing is preferable to a big hip and shoulder turn. One of my pet peeves has been with some golf instruction that advises tight seniors to turn out their right foot in order to make a bigger hip turn. Although this indeed will create a bigger hip turn, it usually unplugs the golfer and dissipates the crucial resistance between the lower and upper body.

No question about it good golf demands flexibility in the upper trunk, primarily in the obliques, lats, chest, and lumbar muscles. Trunk flexibility is probably more important in golf than in any other sport. Golfers with rounded shoulders have a problem because, among other things, rounded shoulders indicate an over-dominance and tightness in the pec muscles, which are required to expand on the backswing. Rounded shoulders basically mean that the front muscles of the chest are too tight and the back muscles are too weak.

7.4. Restricted shoulder turn.

The upper spine in the golf swing rotates approximately 60 percent more on the backswing than the lower spine, so if a person's shoulders are too tight, they won't allow the upper spine to rotate to its maximum. This rounded-shoulder condition, called *thoracic kyphosis*, is commonly seen among seniors and even Champions Tour players, who evolve into this condition, who also eventually end up with very tight hips. This evolution is caused by walking thousands of miles around golf courses, tilting forward in a golf stance (which puts the hips in flexion), hitting millions of golf balls, sitting down in airplanes, driving cars, and so forth. It's no wonder that we see this hunchback position in so many senior golfers.

Having a flexible upper trunk and back can make up for a lot of other physical faults in the golf swing, and makes it much easier to get the arms and club behind the body in the proper sequence. The following drills and stretches will help to increase your shoulder coil.

**Golf Swing Drill**

1. ELBOW-TO-WALL
(D6, page 118)

2. SET, TURN & PLACE DRILL
(D7, page 119)

**Stretches**

1. STANDING DROP-OFF
(S13, page 172)

2. CATS & DOGS
(S24, page 180)

3. DOWNWARD DOG
(S1, page 165)

4. TRIANGLE
(S27, page 181)

5. PSOAS
(S15, page 173)

6. OBLIQUE SIDE FLEXION
(S31, page 184)

7. PRETZEL
(S32, page 185)

8. PECTORALIS
(S37, page 189)

# FAULT NO. 4: LOSS OF SPINE ANGLE

Keeping one's spine angle is paramount for hitting solid and consistent shots. The reason it's so important is because when a golfer comes out of his spine angle (*fig 7.5*), he is really altering the center of gravity and losing energy, plus taking his muscles out of contraction. However, I must make note, that when a golfer stands tall in the address position and actually lowers himself as he starts down, energy is actually increased. This move has been seen in many of golf's greatest players, including Tiger Woods, Byron Nelson and virtually thousands of other players. In fact, I would say that the majority of great players went down into the shot. However, you'll seldom ever see a great player rising up. On the other hand, coming up and out of one's spine angle is very common among high handicappers.

When a golfer rises up as he comes into the ball, the torque and forces are lost and, as a result, the club will be released too soon. This will almost

7.5. A loss of spine angle due to restricted muscles.

invariably result in a hand flip through the ball. Another negative of coming out of the spine angle is that it normally puts the weight back on the heels, consequently taking the brace and stability out of the lower body. There are a few players that "backed out" of their spine angle going through the ball, but that happened only with the driver. Because the ball is teed up, a person can get away with it a little more with the driver than with an iron.

Once again, having a very stable and mobile body (especially lower body) will nearly always ensure maintaining a level spine angle.

Here are some drills and stretches to help maintain your spine angle.

## Golf Swing Drill

1. BRUSH-THE-GRASS
(D15, page 129)

2. FLAGSTICK
(D20, page 133)

## Stretches

1. COUNTER
(S23, page 179)

2. DOWNWARD DOG
(S1, page 165)

3. RUNNERS
(S3, page 166)

4. EXTENDED LATERAL
(S28, page 182)

5. SPREAD-FOOT FORWARD BEND
(S2, page 165)

6. PSOAS
(S15, page 173)

7. HIP-THIGH EXTENSIONS
(S19, page 176

8. LATERAL BALL ROLLS
(S42, page 193)

9. WALL SQUATS
(S46, page 197)

## FAULT NO. 5: FLYING ELBOWS AND CHICKEN WINGS

A flying right elbow (made famous by Jack Nicklaus, Fred Couples and others) isn't necessarily a bad thing (*fig* 7.6). The elbow and arm function are dictated by how a person's scapula (or shoulder blade) is built. In other words, the rhomboid muscles play a vital role in how the scapula functions. In addition, people with thick chests normally have thick backs and therefore don't have a lot of range of motion in their shoulder blades. Remember that the shoulders control the arms, and the arms control the hands. Thick chests also inhibit a golfer's arms from folding naturally and easily. With a lack of shoulder-blade rotation, the arms tend to lift or stray away from the body.

Golfers whose backs and chests aren't as broad tend to keep their elbows closer to their sides. One of Nicklaus' concerns was that sometimes his right elbow would fly too much and cause him to lift up out of his backswing. When this occurred, his head would rise and his left heel would also come up too high off of the ground. Consequently, his left foot would come crashing down prematurely and he would be prone to hit a pull hook. (Obviously this didn't happen too much to him.)

7.6. Fred Couples is living proof that flying right elbows aren't necessarily a bad thing.

Chicken wings on the through swing occur in much the same was as a flying elbow on the backswing, again due to muscle restrictions in the upper torso and, especially the shoulders. What generally happens is the left side of the body doesn't shift and rotate out of the way, which causes the arms to crash into the blocked torso, forcing them to collapse. In other words, the chicken wing is actually a result of the lack of rotation of the upper torso and shoulder joints. The fact is people with tight lats, obliques, and impinged shoulders are very prone to the dreaded chicken wing. People are forever trying to put towels and gloves under their left armpits, using

*Secrets of Golf Instruction and Flexibility*

straps and many other remedies to stay connected. These aids may help some, but the *best* way to cure this problem is to go to the source and loosen up the main muscles that are creating the problem in the first place. These drills and stretches should help get to the root of the problem.

## Golf Swing Drills

1. ARM-CONNECTION
(D19, page 132)

2. RIGHT-ARM-ONLY
(D12, page 125)

## Stretches

1. STANDING DROP-OFF
(S13, page 172)

2. OVERHEAD EXTENSION
(S36, page 188)

3. DOWNWARD DOG
(S1, page 165)

4. PSOAS
(S15, page 173)

5. RUSSIAN BALL TWIST
(S35, page 188)

6. LATERAL BALL ROLLS
(S42, page 193)

7. INT. & EXT. SHOULDER ROTATORS
(S43, page 194)

8. WHY ME'S & BREAST STROKE
(S40 & S41, pages 192-193)

7.7. Over the top.

7.8. Getting stuck on the right side.

## FAULT NO. 6: DOWNSWING PROBLEMS

These are 5 common downswing faults:

1.  Over the top (*fig 7.7*)

2.  Lack of lower body stability

3.  Getting stuck on the right side

4.  Straightening the legs

5.  Upper body starting down first

Without question, how we come into the ball is *the* most important aspect of the swing and truly is the make-or-break moment. We must initiate the downswing with the unwinding of the hips. In fact, there really is no top of the backswing because the hips actually begin unwinding a split second before the club reaches the top. This move actually *increases* the X factor on the backswing and is a common trait among the power hitters.

As the hips are unwinding, the center of gravity moves forward as the weight shifts onto the left foot. The forces on the foot then create a shock wave that rushes back up the femur, causing the hips to clear. When the hips begin the process of starting down, the chain reaction begins; the upper trunk unwinds, the arms and club drop down between the right shoulder and the right hip, and finally the hands follow into impact. The result of this sequencing creates centrifugal force, which causes the wrists to lag behind the arms and body, storing up maximum power for the release yet to come. However, if this sequencing is out of order, there will be an interruption of the synchronization of these body parts. If the upper body starts down first (and not the lower), the hips usually will come to a crashing halt far too soon, creating a premature uncocking of the wrists, and often the aforementioned chicken wing (*fig 7.8*).

Here are some drills and stretches to create a maximum lower body move into the ball, and help shift the weight and clear the hips.

## Golf Swing Drills

1. STEP-ON-THE-GAS
(D13, page 127)

2. RIGHT-ARM-ONLY
(D12, page 125)

3. WALL-PRESS
(D16, page 130)

4. BASEBALL
(D8 page 120)

## Stretches

1. CATS & DOGS
(S24, page 180)

2. COBRA
(S26, page 181)

3. DOWNWARD DOG
(S1, page 165)

4. WARRIOR II
(S16, page 174)

5. TRIANGLE
(S27, page 181)

6. EXTENDED LATERAL
(S28, page 182)

7. PRETZEL IN CHAIR
(S32A, page 186)

8. AIR BENCH
(S4, page 166)

As strange as this may sound, having tight pecs or a tight upper torso also will cause the chicken wing because of the chest's lack of capacity to expand and properly rotate on the backswing, which will not allow the Push Pull sequence to occur. Again, the transition sequence from the top of the swing down, is the make-or-break moment in the golf swing.

7.9. Premature straightening of the left leg.

7.10. Hogan's *soft* knees allowed a smooth weight transfer.

## Straightening Of The Legs

Like every other sport, golf is a lower body game. Although the vast majority of golf instruction centers on upper-body swing mechanics and swing positions, the lower-body stability allows the upper body to do its thing. One such swing fault that is guaranteed to disrupt the stabilization of the golf swing is a premature straightening of the legs, especially the left leg, as the golfer transitions into the downswing (*fig* 7.9). This locking up causes a braking motion that disrupts the rhythm and forces as they flow into impact.

A lot of teachers advocate a straightening of the left leg at impact to generate more shock power through the shot. I have no problem with this, except that it is a highly skilled move that requires precise timing. The vast majority of amateur golfers simply can't perform this move with precision. Keeping the knees flexed through the shot is almost considered taboo by many of today's teachers, but guys like Nelson, Hogan (*fig* 7.10), Nicklaus, Bolt, Knudson, Johnny Miller, Palmer, never straightened their legs, and as a result were some of the greatest shot makers and players in history.

To further clarify, the left knee anatomically must get at least over and above the left foot before any kind of straightening occurs. As long as that happens, it doesn't matter what the left leg does. When the left knee gets over and on top of the left foot, you've got it!

*Secrets of Golf Instruction and Flexibility*

Here are a set of sequenced flexibility exercises to allow your legs to maintain stability and mobility. (These drills are also applicable for straightening the legs on the backswing as indicated in Fault No. 1, Poor Address and Takeaway Problems.)

**Golf Swing Drills**

1. LEFT-LEG PIVOT
(D14, page 128)

2. PULLBACK
(D4, page 114)

**Stretches**

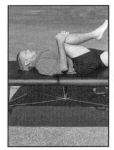   

1. SINGLE-LEG PELVIC TILT
(S5, page 167)

2. DOUBLE-LEG PELVIC TILT
(S6, page 167)

3. STRAIGHT-LEG HAMSTRING
(S9, page 169)

4. ADDUCTOR
(S10, page 169)

5. ABDUCTOR
(S11, page 170)

6. PSOAS
(S15, page 173)

7. RUSSIAN BALL TWIST
(S35, page 188)

8. QUADRICEPS
(S12, page 171)

9. HIP CROSS-OVERS
(S20, page 177)

## FAULT NO. 7: ABBREVIATED FINISH

A simple comparison of the finish of a tour player with a high handicapper usually tells the whole story. The overwhelming majority of tour players finish completely on their left sides and, in most cases, with their chests aiming to the left of the target (*fig* 7.11). The higher handicapper seldom comes close to this full finish position, usually ending up with an abbreviated finish or incomplete follow-through.

Most golfers lack the necessary flexibility to finish all the way around (*fig* 7.12), the same way they lack the flexibility to get into a perfect backswing position. The golf swing drills and stretches on the following page will help you accomplish a full finish.

7.11. David Duval completely "unwound."

## SUMMARY

All the drills and stretches recommended in this chapter will help you correct your golf swing faults and build a much more fundamentally sound golf swing, both physically and mechanically. They will help you be able to do what you and your instructor are trying to accomplish in your swing.

The exercises connected with these specific drills should not be used as a substitute for your entire flexibility program, but rather as an addendum. Always regard your daily program (outlined in Chapter 10) as your main staple for flexibility conditioning and for better golf.

7.12. Abbreviated follow through.

# Golf Swing Drills

1. RIGHT-ARM-ONLY
(D12, page 125)

2. DICK MAYER
(D9, page 122)

3. FLAGSTICK
(D20, page 133)

# Stretches

1. CATS & DOGS
(S24, page 180)

2. DOWNWARD
DOG
(S1, page 165)

3. TRIANGLE
(S27, page 181)

4. PSOAS
(S15 page 173)

5. OBLIQUE SIDE
FLEXION
(S31, page 184)

6. RUSSIAN BALL
TWIST
(S35, page 188)

7. LATERAL BALL
ROLLS
(S42, page 193)

8. PECTORALIS
(S37, page 189)

9. INT. & EXT.
SHOULDER
ROTATORS
(S43, page 194)

# *Drills*

This chapter contains drills that are specific to different segments of the golf swing. The best way to utilize the drills is to practice them along with your flexibility program. As your flexibility improves, the drills will become more effective and definitely accelerate your progress to a freer and more powerful golf swing.

## ADDRESS AND STABILITY DRILLS

### D1. Close-the-Eyes Balance Drill

**Benefit:** Practicing this drill, even during your round, will help you achieve a balanced address position.

**Step 1.** Take a golf club (as shown in *fig* 8.1) and get into your address position. Close your eyes and pay specific attention to where your weight is on your feet, e.g., heels, toe, balls of feet, insides, outsides.

**Step 2.** Make sure your weight is 50-50 on each foot, and that the majority of your weight (about 60

8.1. Weight 50-50 on each foot, with the majority on the balls of the feet.

8.2. Bend from hips, allowing your arms to hang softly. The hip joint should be directly in line with the ankle.

percent) is on the balls of your feet with just a slight amount on the heels and toes (*fig* 8.2).

Your arms should hang straight down and, if you let go of the club, it should land just outside your toe line. If you do this drill without a club, clap your hands. This will put you into perfect balance, and you'll be ready to go.

## D2. Barefoot Balance Drill

**Benefit:** Mastering this drill pays great dividends in your golf swing, because maintaining balance in the lower body will eliminate many swing faults that occur in the upper body.

8.3. Address position.

8.4. Weight on ball of right foot.

**Step 1.** Stand barefoot (on grass) in your address position, paying strict attention to where the weight and weight pressure are on your feet (*fig* 8.3). The weight should be 50–50 on each foot, with the majority on the balls of your feet.

**Step 2.** Go ahead and swing. (You can hit a ball during this drill.) Pay attention to where the weight and *weight pressure* are on your feet as you shift during your swing. On the backswing, the majority of your weight should go onto the ball of the right foot (*fig* 8.4), and, on the forward swing, the weight should shift to the ball of the left foot (*fig* 8.5) and then immediately toward your heel (*fig* 8.6). You'll be able to quickly determine if your weight distribution is in balance.

8.5. Weight shifts onto the ball of the left foot.

8.6. Weight finishes on the left foot toward the heel.

*Drills*

8.7. Address position on one-half foam roller.

8.8. Weight shifts onto ball of right foot.

### D3. Foam-Roller Drill

**Benefit:** This outstanding drill helps eliminate excess rotation or sliding in your swing. You'll need a one-half foam roller for this drill.

**Step 1.** Take your golf stance on a one-half foam roller, making sure that you're perfectly balanced (*fig* 8.7). Try not to let your toes or heels touch the ground. Depending on the size of the foam roller, they may touch; if so, keep the weight very light on the toes and heels.

**Step 2.** Make some golf swings, feeling the weight go back onto the ball of your right foot (*fig* 8.8), then back onto your left foot (*figs* 8.9 and 8.10). Make sure that your hips turn as you shift onto your left foot, maintaining balance. You can also place an impact bag perpendicular to your left foot and swing into it (*fig* 8.11).

8.9. Weight onto ball of left foot.

8.10. Follow-through.

8.11. Alternate: impact bag perpendicular to left foot.

## D4. Pullback Drill

Benefit: Mastery of this three part drill helps eliminate excessive movements in the golf swing and helps develop lower body stability. This is the most common and effective drill of all the drills I use.

**Step 1.** Tee the ball up slightly with an 8 iron. Take your setup and pretend that you're standing in dried concrete and that your legs are completely frozen (*fig* 8.12).

**Step 2**. On the backswing, swing the club upward while keeping your lower body as braced as possible (*fig* 8.13). (Try to keep your belt buckle pointing at the ball.) I frequently videotape my students while they perform this drill, and they're always amazed at how much they've

8.12. Part 1, Setup as if in dried concrete.

8.13. Part 2, Backswing with lower body braced.

*Secrets of Golf Instruction and Flexibility*

still turned and rotated at the top of their swings, since they feel that they haven't moved at all.

**Step 3**. From the top of your restricted backswing, swing your arms down through the ball and into the finish (*fig* 8.14) without moving your lower body. Make sure that you keep your right foot flat as you swing through.

**Step 4**. From the finish of your arm swing, pull (swing) the shaft back to the original address position (*fig* 8.15).

The secret of this drill is to keep the right foot flat on the ground throughout the entire swing. After hitting five good shots, you can graduate to Part II of the Pullback drill (D4A, p.116).

8.14. Part 3, Swing through the ball.

8.15. Part 4, Swing the club back to the ball.

8.16. Right foot on its toe with chest facing left of target.

## D4A. Part II, Pullback Drill

**Step 1.** For Part II of the Pullback Drill, repeat Part I (*fig* 8.12 and 8.13). (Try not to turn your hips.)

**Step 2.** Now, instead of freezing your lower body as you swing down, go ahead and let your body release as you swing into a full finish. In other words, you can release your right foot now. Be sure to swing your arms all the way around with your right foot up on its toe, and your chest facing left of the target (*fig* 8.16). Repeat this drill until you hit five good shots. In other words, think "*no back-swing with the hips, and all forward swing.*"

## D4B. Part III, Pullback Drill

After you've hit five good shots on Parts I and II of this drill, now you are ready for Part III (*fig* 8.17-8.19). Now, however, instead of keeping your torso as still as possible on the backswing, go ahead and shift your weight slightly onto the ball of your right foot and let your left shoulder

8.17. Address Position.

8.18. Weight shifted slightly onto ball of right foot.

8.19. Make a normal weight shift through the shot.

come under your chin (*fig* 8.18). In other words, make a more normal backswing with your upper body (still keeping your lower body restricted), then swing down and through the shot into the finish (*fig* 8.19).

## BACKSWING DRILLS

### D5. Push-Away Drill

**Benefit:** This drill gets the weight shifting and the club moving back on a straight path. You'll need a head cover, plastic water bottle, or any other suitable object for this drill.

8.20. Address position with head cover behind club head.

8.21. Sweep away the object.

**Step 1.** Address a ball with a water bottle or a head cover placed directly behind the club head (*fig* 8.20).

**Step 2.** Sweep the object away as you move into your backswing (*fig* 8.21). You'll feel a smooth weight shift into your right foot.

### D6. Elbow-to-Wall Drill

**Benefit:** This drill focuses on the turn and helps teach you the uninterrupted flow you should feel in your upper trunk.

**Step 1.** Stand six to eight inches away from a wall or post. Make a fist with your left hand, letting your thumb stick out. Now place your thumb into the middle of your sternum (*fig* 8.22).

8.22. Thumb placed into sternum.

8.23. Left elbow touching wall.

*Secrets of Golf Instruction and Flexibility*

**Step 2.** Keeping your forearm level, simply turn your upper torso until your left elbow touches the wall, while making sure you stay in your spine angle (*fig* 8.23). Make sure that the gap between your right thigh and the wall stays constant. In other words, don't let your right hip slide into the wall. (If it does, you probably have tight hips.)

## D7. Set, Turn, and Place Drill

**Benefit:** This drill synchronizes the arms, torso, and club, putting you into a balanced position at the top of your swing.

**Step 1.** Stand in a balanced address position. While maintaining your posture and spine angle, simply fold your arms and set the shaft on your right shoulder (*fig* 8.24).

**Step 2.** Keeping the shaft on your shoulder and staying in your spine angle, make a relaxed shoulder turn (*fig* 8.25).

**Step 3.** Now, extend your arms away from your torso (*fig* 8.26).

8.24. Place shaft on right shoulder.

8.25. Turn shoulders.

8.26. Extend arms away from torso.

## D8. Baseball Drill

**Benefit:** This drill will help you develop a proper weight shift throughout your swing. This drill is especially helpful for people who have trouble shifting their weight properly in the takeaway.

**Step 1.** Assume your stance as you address the ball (*fig* 8.27). You're not going to hit it just yet.

**Step 2.** Swing back and shift your weight onto your right foot. As you shift back, lift your left foot off of the ground (toward your right knee) so that you're completely balanced on your right foot (*fig* 8.28). Stay there for a moment, allowing your body to feel the balance point. Repeat this two times (*fig* 8.29).

8.27. Address the ball.

8.28. Weight shifted on right side, left foot lifted.

8.29. Repeat Steps 1 and 2 twice.

**Step 3.** Keeping the "feel" of your weight shift into your right side, swing back again (*fig* 8.30). This time, keep your left foot down on the backswing and swing through into the finish (*fig* 8.31 and *fig* 8.32). Once you get back to the right side and you're loaded and in balance, almost everything else is secondary. It happens almost automatically.

8.30. Keep left foot down.

8.31. Downswing shifting weight to left side.

8.32. Follow through.

## D9. Dick Mayer Drill

Dick Mayer, the 1957 U.S. Open Champion and 1957 World Open Champion, taught me this drill. Mayer learned the drill from Ben Hogan, when the two of them used to practice together in Fort Worth in the fall, getting ready for the next year.

According to Dick, Hogan hit thousands of balls using this drill. He would simply cock his wrists so that his left hand was opposite his right thigh and his shaft was parallel to the ground. From there, he would pump the club with a very restricted backswing and hit through the shot with an aggressive, full motion. Hogan told Mayer he wanted to eliminate any excessive length and overswinging in his backswing. When he first became a pro, Hogan had a long backswing and was often unable to control it. He tightened his backswing, and this drill was one way that he kept it that way.

**Benefit:** This is a great drill for eliminating excessive backswing movements.

**Step 1.** Start by cocking your wrists so that the back of the left hand is directly opposite the right thigh, with the shaft parallel to the ground and parallel to the target line (*fig* 8.33).

8.33. Step 1, Set shaft parallel to the ground.

8.34. Step 2, Pump the club slightly.

8.35. Step 3, Swing through the shot.

**Step 2.** Simply pump the club slightly on the backswing (*fig* 8.34) and swing on through the shot (*fig* 8.35).

## D10. Bruce Summerhays Drill

I used to see Bruce start every practice session with this drill.

**Benefit:** The upper body in the golf swing is a blending of a torso turn, an arm swing, and wrist cock. Many golfers have difficulty blending all these elements together. This drill helps synchronize these body parts and will enable them to achieve a more fluid motion, particularly helping you feel the action of the wrists. Many people are intimidated to try this drill because they feel a lack of control with the club placed above the ball, but after doing it a couple of times they are usually amazed at how well they can hit the ball.

**Step 1.** Start in your address position with the shaft fully cocked, so that it's parallel to the ground and straight out in front of you (*fig* 8.36).

**Step 2.** Swing back and hit the ball (*fig* 8.37 and 8.38).

8.36. Step 1, Shaft parallel to the ground.

8.37. Step 2, Swing back.

8.38. Step 3, Hit the ball.

8.39. Address position.

8.40. Stop at the top for a moment.

8.41. Follow through.

## D11. Stop-at-the-Top Drill

Even perfect mechanics won't do you any good if you don't have balance, rhythm, and timing. Undoubtedly, the most important move in the golf swing is the transition from the top of the swing down into impact. If you start down too soon with the hands or the upper body at the top of the backswing instead of allowing your lower body to initiate the downswing motion, the odds of hitting a good shot are greatly diminished.

**Benefit:** This drill will teach you to overcome the temptation of starting down too quickly, and help you develop a slight pause at the top of the swing which will enable your lower body to unwind first, improving your rhythm and timing.

**Step 1.** Address the ball (*fig* 8.39).

**Step 2.** Swing back to the top of your backswing and come to a complete stop (*fig* 8.40). Hold it there for two seconds.

**Step 3.** Now return to the address position and repeat Step 2.

**Step 4.** Make a normal swing. Now, you'll feel the temptation to start down too soon, only it'll be replaced by a nice hesitant pause at the top (*fig* 8.41).

# FORWARD-SWING DRILLS

## D12. Right-Arm-Only Drill No. 1

**Benefit:** This drill is designed to teach you the proper feel of shifting your weight and clearing your left side as you swing through the shot.

**Step 1.** Take out a 6 iron or 7 iron, turn it upside down, and grip it just above the hosel with your right hand. Place the shaft behind you (*fig* 8.42) as if you were going to throw it down the fairway. This shouldn't be hard since many of us have probably done that after hitting a bad shot!

**Step 2.** Swing the shaft forward (*fig* 8.43 and 8.44) and make the shaft "whoosh" on the front left side of your body. You should feel a smooth weight shift, release, and rotation through the motion.

8.42. Turn iron upside down and grip just above the hosel.

8.43. Step forward while swinging the right arm.

8.44. Make the shaft whoosh.

## Advanced Right-Arm-Only Drill (D12A)

The Advanced Right-Arm-Only drill is similar, only now we're really going to hit a ball with the right arm only. Most golfers don't shift their weight to the left side and instead hang back, which keeps the center of gravity behind the ball and can create a swing that is out of control. Pay attention to how solidly you hit the ball. Solid is good.

**Step 1.** Tee up a ball relatively low to the ground. Take a normal grip with your right hand slightly choked down on the grip.

**Step 2.** Place the club above and in front of the ball, with the shaft parallel to the ground (*fig* 8.45).

**Step 3.** Swing back to the top (*fig* 8.46) and then back down, actually hitting the ball. The secret of success with this drill is to make a *concentrated effort to shift your weight forward during the downswing* (*fig* 8.47). If you don't shift your weight forward but instead hang back on your right side, this drill will be difficult to perform.

8.45. Club shaft above and in front of the ball.

8.46. Swing back to the top.

8.47. Weight shifted forward.

# D13. Step-on-the-Gas Drill

**Benefit:** Most golfers fail to shift their weight properly onto the left foot on the forward swing, instead either straightening the left leg too early, or hanging back on the right foot. Doing either causes a golfer to lose power and consistency.

This drill will help you shift your lower body forward on the downswing. You'll probably find that paying more attention to the forward swing will automatically help put you into a better position on the backswing.

**Step 1.** Pretend that there's a gas pedal (accelerator) under your left foot. To get a better visual, you can take a towel or other flat object and place it underneath your left foot (*fig* 8.48).

8.48. Imaginary gas pedal under left foot.

8.49. Left knee flexed until weight hits left foot.

---

**Step 2.** As you start your downswing, "step on the gas" by trying to get 90 percent of your weight to hit the ball of the left foot before the club gets to the ball. To do this properly, start shifting your "flexed" left knee and hip onto your left foot, making sure you don't let your upper body move out in front as you do so (*fig* 8.49).

### D14. Left-Leg Pivot Drill

**Benefit:** This drill will help you feel the rotation of the hips and shoulders through the ball while stabilizing on a solid left side, and also allow you to feel your right side release.

**Step 1.** Get a 7 iron or 8 iron. Take an address position, with the ball slightly forward of middle in your stance. Drop your right foot behind you so that you're up on your toes and balancing primarily on your left leg only (*fig* 8.50).

**Step 2.** Swing back and swing through (*figs* 8.51 and 8.52). As you start down, consciously try to rotate your left hip and shoulder through the shot. You should almost feel that you're coming over the top with your shoulders, but you won't be because your left hip will be stabilized.

8.50. Right foot on toes, balancing primarily on left leg.

8.51. Swing back...

8.52. ...and through.

*Secrets of Golf Instruction and Flexibility*

# D15. Brush-the-Grass Drill

**Benefit:** This drill will help you develop the proper feel of the left side rotating out of the way as well as staying in your spine angle.

**Step 1.** Take your address position while placing your right arm away from your body (*fig* 8.53). Let your left arm hang softly, or bring it up to your chest.

**Step 2.** Simply swing down with your right hand and arm, imagining that you're going to brush the grass with your right hand (*fig* 8.54).

8.53. Backswing with right arm away from body.

8.54. Swing down with right arm as if you were going to brush the grass.

8.55. Press your forearm and hand into the wall.

8.56. Apply pressure in the feet, thighs, and hips.

## D16. Wall-Press Drill

**Benefit:** This is a lower-body exercise. Mastery of it will do wonders for properly moving your lower body into the shot.

**Step 1.** Facing the corner of a wall or doorway, get into a golf stance and place your right hand into the wall so that your forearm is parallel to the floor and applying force into the wall (*fig* 8.55).

**Step 2.** Firmly press your hand and arm into the wall, and apply extra pressure into the ball of your left foot while your right foot presses forward. You should also feel your thighs pressing, and you'll notice that your hips will automatically begin turning (*fig* 8.56). You should feel a lot of torque on the outside of your left hip. This is precisely what the lower body should feel like as you shift and turn into the ball.

## D17. Power-Fan Drill

**Benefit:** This drill will help strengthen your body, create power, and increase your two-cheek position. Combined with a flexibility program, swinging the fan is a great training aide.

**Step 1.** Get into a proper address position. While in your address position, cock the wrists and place the power fan just outside your right thigh with the fan approximately parallel to the ground and parallel to the target line (*fig* 8.57).

**Step 2.** Pump the fan by going into a modified backswing (*fig* 8.58), and then swing it through, making the fan whoosh in the front and on the left side of

8.57. Set fan with your hands just outside your thigh.

8.58. Modified backswing.

8.59. Swing the fan, creating a whoosh.

8.60. Swing the fan to the left of the target.

your body (*fig* 8.59 and *fig* 8.60). The wings of the fan create wind resistance, and you're going to have to use some extra effort to really make it whoosh.

# D18. Impact-Bag Drill

**Benefit:** Swinging into an impact bag teaches the proper movement patterns into the ball.

You will need an impact bag for this drill.

**Step 1.** Take a normal address position with the club behind the impact bag (*fig* 8.61).

**Step 2.** Swing into the bag, making sure to shift your weight forward as you swing (*fig* 8.62).

If you want to learn to draw the ball, simply turn the toe of the club into the bag as you swing into it, and hold the club face open for a soft fade.

8.61. Take a normal backswing.

8.62. Swing and shift your weight into the bag.

8.63. Towel underneath left armpit.

8.64. Rotate through the shot keeping the towel tucked under your armpit.

### D19. Arm-Connection Drill

**Benefit:** This drill is very effective in helping the arms work in sync with the torso. It is especially helpful in eliminating the dreaded chicken wing.

You'll need a towel or head cover for this drill.

**Step 1.** Put a towel or head cover underneath the left armpit (*fig* 8.63).

**Step 2.** Take some three-quarter swings, making sure that the towel stays tucked under the armpit (*fig* 8.64). If the towel falls out, your swing has gotten too "arm-ee." Make sure that you rotate your hips and shoulders through the shot as you swing through. Go ahead and hit balls with this drill.

8.65. Flag on shoulders behind head with majority on right side.

8.66. Turning back.

8.67. Swing through making the flag whoosh.

# ROTATION DRILLS

## D20. Flagstick Drill

**Benefit:** This simple drill teaches the proper rotation of the hips and shoulders and helps maintain your spine angle throughout your swing.

You will need a flagstick or long pole for this drill.

**Step 1.** Lay a flagstick on your shoulders behind your head. Make sure the flag and the majority of the pole is on the right side (*fig* 8.65).

**Step 2.** Get into your stance and simply turn back (*fig* 8.66). At the top of your backswing the end of the flagstick should be pointing about 14" outside the imaginary ball. Swing through, making the flag whoosh at the same spot (*fig* 8.67).

8.68. Place a 5 iron across chest with club head parallel to spine and the toe facing upward.

8.69. Backswing.

8.70. Forward swing.

### D21. Upper-Thorax Drill

**Benefit:** This simple drill teaches the proper shoulder rotation in the golf swing.

**Step 1.** Place a 5 iron across your chest up around your shoulders (*fig* 8.68). Make sure that the toe of the club is facing upward and parallel to your spine.

**Step 2.** Hold the club in place and make a backswing (*fig* 8.69) and forward swing (*fig* 8.70), imagining that you're hitting the ball with the head of the 5 iron.

# Anatomy of Common Swing Theories

## *(and Other Myths)*

Unlike any other sport, golf has had more swing tips and theories than possibly all other sports combined, not to mention that many of them are contrary to one another. I've actually seen golf publications with conflicting tips from different golf professionals in the same magazine. One such magazine had a swing tip that encouraged people to take the club back in a one-piece takeaway, while later in the same publication, another pro encouraged people to set the wrists early. Who is the reader to believe? It's no wonder why this game has turned so many people into basket cases.

Yet, as we've discussed before, nobody can really prove if their theory is really THE correct theory for any individual. In all seriousness, as a teaching professional for years, I've lost track of how many students got so obsessed and confused about this game that many have *literally* gone to see a psychologist to get straightened out (which is interesting, because I've had several students that are "shrinks," and a couple of them were just as confused as my other students).

Having studied the game from both the golf instruction side as well as the physiological side, I'd like to give a true unbiased look at several common golf swing tips and theories from an anatomical perspective.

## KEEPING THE HEAD STILL
This swing tip has been around since bored sheepherders began hitting rocks around the pasture with their crooks. Very few golfers in history actually kept their heads perfectly still, but a few of the all-time greats did.

9.1. A slight rotation of the upper spine and head allows a smooth weight transfer.

9.2. Keeping the head still retards a proper weight shift.

These include Arnold Palmer, Jack Nicklaus, Bobby Jones, and Freddie Couples, to name a *few*. I've actually shown Arnold Palmer many videos of his swing throughout different periods of his career where his head did move, and he adamantly maintains that those videos were "bad" swings he just happened to make at the time. I do admit, however, that for most of his career he did keep his head still.

The truth is that the overwhelming majority of great players do move their heads. Since the head is connected to the spine, and the upper spine rotates over to the right side, it's only natural that the head rotates along with it (*fig* 9.1). The Creator designed us to have two pivot points—a left and right hip. By keeping the head still, the upper body weight isn't allowed to shift naturally into the right hip, therefore retarding an efficient weight transfer (*fig* 9.2). Although keeping the head still does help prevent excess movement in the swing, a serious problem usually evolves; that is, preventing the weight from loading properly into the hips puts a tremendous strain on the fascia in one's lower back. Over time, this will usually lead to back pain. The guys who kept their heads still, e.g., Palmer, Nicklaus, and Couples, invariably suffered back problems throughout their careers. When the weight properly loads onto the hips, the friction is taken off the fascia and the other joints of the body.

## KEEPING THE LEFT WRIST FLAT

There have been great players throughout history who played with cupped wrists (*fig* 9.3), flat wrists (*fig* 9.4), and even convex wrists (*fig* 9.5). Most teachers, however, seem to prefer a flat left wrist.

The position of your wrist at the top of the swing normally depends on two factors: the thickness of your musculature around your wrists, and how you grip the club, i.e., either in a strong, weak, or neutral manner.

*Secrets of Golf Instruction and Flexibility*

9.3. Freddie Couples' cupped wrist.

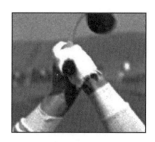

9.4. Jack Nicklaus' flat wrist.

9.5. Lee Trevino's convex wrist.

Generally speaking, people who are thick-chested and on the chunky side, tend to have a flat or convex wrist at the top. Conversely, people who are slender and have skinnier wrists tend to cup their wrists a little more. As far as the grip, people who have strong grips tend to cup it more (since the hand is turned over, and in a sense, is already cupped), and golfers who have neutral or even weak grips, tend to have their wrists flat.

Unless your hand position at the top is extreme one way or the other, or is causing you a lot of problems with the position of your club face, I wouldn't worry about it very much.

## UPRIGHT SWINGS OR FLAT SWINGS

Ben Hogan and Jack Nicklaus were the two greatest players of their time. Hogan had a flat swing plane (*fig* 9.6), Jack an upright one (*fig* 9.7). There has been a lot of controversy on which way is *the* best way. If one way was better than the other, then one of those guys was doing it wrong. I don't think so! Jim Hardy, who is a friend of mine, has authored one of the most successful books and videos of the last decade called *The Plane Truth about the Golf Swing*. Jim feels that, in theory, the one-plane swing is the most effective way to swing and, as a result, legions of golfers have switched over to that method. What is often overlooked is that Jim has also said that "most" people are better off using a two-plane swing, simply because to swing in one plane, one needs superb flexibility.

9.6. Ben Hogan's flatter swing plane.

9.7. Jack Nicklaus' upright swing plane.

I agree with Jim that a one-plane swing in theory is probably the best way to go about it, but to get an efficient one-plane swing, a person has to have a much steeper shoulder turn. Hogan, for example, stood very tall at address and dipped down quite a bit, which made it easier to get his left arm in line with his shoulder plane. In other words, the more the left shoulder goes down, the easier it is for the left arm to get on plane. Arnold Palmer also turned his shoulders on a steep angle, and he was probably the poster boy for the one-plane swing. However, the more the shoulders flatten out, the harder it is to get the arms on plane with them, and instead they'll tend to lift up.

What I'm saying is that since most people don't possess enough flexibility to tilt their shoulders deeply, they therefore shouldn't be trying to do something their bodies can't do effectively.

In summary, people who are more slender and possess ample flexibility can give the one-plane swing a try. Shorter, stockier people who are not very flexible are usually better off using a two-plane system.

*Secrets of Golf Instruction and Flexibility*

9.8. Jim Furyk releasing his right side.

9.9. High handicapper stuck on right side.

## KEEPING THE RIGHT FOOT
## FLAT THROUGH IMPACT

A fairly recent swing tip over the last few years has been to keep the right foot flat through impact. This has become popular with the evolution of the modern swing, where many teachers emphasize less leg action. The reason behind this is to curb the player from driving the legs too much, which usually gets the club head stuck behind him. This is accurate, but I think this swing tip should be reserved for tour players and better golfers. Tour pros play a lot of shots in the wind, and as a result, often get into the habit of driving into the shot too much, that is, trapping the ball. Plus, the modern swing incorporates a narrower stance, so there's much less need or room to drive the legs.

For the average player, in fact for many golfers, it's not a good road to travel. The main difference between tour players and average high handicappers is that tour players get to their left sides (*fig* 9.8) and high handicappers stay stuck back on their right sides (*fig* 9.9), which inevitably leads to a hand flip through the ball. It doesn't make much sense to try to get high handicappers

---

*Anatomy of Common Swing Theories*

to keep their right foot flat when they're already stuck on their back foot. For decades, one of the most successful swing tips, especially made popular by "The Silver Scot" Tommy Armour, was to kick the right knee and foot in toward the ball to start the downswing. For years, Gary Player would actually walk through to the target by taking a step down the fairway, and he certainly is one of the greatest players who ever lived.

Another reason the right foot comes off the ground is because the left hip pulls it off due to its rotation through the shot. Thus, players endanger stunting their hip rotation by anchoring down that right foot.

Unless you're good enough to really work your shots like a tour player, my advice is to "let that foot go!"

## RETURN TO THE ADDRESS POSITION AT IMPACT

This swing tip has always been one of my all-time pet peeves. Many teachers taught it to me throughout the years, mainly in the 1960's and 1970's. Unfortunately I actually believed it and got to the point where I perfected it!

9.10. Rotating through the ball—YES!

9.11. Return to the address position—NO!

*Secrets of Golf Instruction and Flexibility*

Most instructors now know better. This theory stated that at impact the hips and shoulders should be parallel to the target line, approximating where they were at address. After video cameras proved that the hips and shoulders were clearly open at impact (*fig* 9.10 and 9.11), many teachers jumped on the bandwagon and conceded that the hips should be cleared *but* that the shoulders should remain square, or parallel to the target line. I once read where one world-renowned instructor actually wanted the placket of one's shirt to aim right of the ball at impact! During one of my seminars on anatomical function in the golf swing at one of his golf schools, he had me removed from the stage because he felt that I was preaching blasphemy when I explained how the hips and shoulders must be open at impact to create centrifugal force.

The fear that instructors have about allowing their students to have their shoulders open at impact is that by condoning this they feel that this will encourage golfers to "come over the top." This is a *very* valid concern, but what really is responsible for clearing the shoulders is the rotation of the left hip. As explained in Chapter 3, in order to get the hips to turn "properly," the lower body must shift over to the front foot first! The lateral shifting of the weight actually drops the shaft into the slot *before the shoulders have cleared!* If the left knee, leg, and hip are solidly on the left foot and have gotten there first, you can't turn the shoulders enough!

Even as recently as this year, I've had vigorous debates with instructors who told me that the shoulders still need to be square at impact, even while they were looking at videos that clearly showed that every great player's hips and shoulders were open at impact. When I pointed this out to them on video, their excuse was that the modern day tour player doesn't swing like that anymore. The player we were looking at was none other than Tiger Woods, so perhaps they figured that Tiger—and **every** great player and ball striker in history—has been doing it wrong!

Thanks to 3D motion capture systems, we've been able to quantify this position and have definite ranges that apply to the overwhelming majority of tour players. On irons at impact, the hips of tour players range from 35 to 50 degrees open, and the shoulders vary from 26 to 34 degrees open. With drivers the ranges are very similar, and in many cases more so.

To prove this, simply pick up a baseball bat or tennis racket and make a few swings, then take an object like a rock, or baseball and throw it underhand-sidearm. Notice how your left hip and shoulder naturally shift and clear out of the way and allow a nice free follow-through of your arms. Now make some swings (or throws), only this time don't let your hips and shoulders open but keep them parallel to the target line. You'll notice that when you don't clear your hips and shoulders, your arms will jam up. It won't take long for you to determine which of these methods is the proper action.

If anyone ever tells you to return to the address position at impact with your hips and shoulders square to the target line, run for the hills! The only thing that should return to the address position at impact is the clubface.

## DEALING WITH FLYING ELBOWS

This swing "fault" has been around forever and has always been considered taboo. Virtually thousands of golfers have practiced with handkerchiefs under their right armpit or straps around the upper arms to keep their arms connected.

Then came Jack Nicklaus with a flying right elbow. Flying elbows can be a bad thing, but they can also be a good thing if they're indigenous to your body type. Just ask Jack, Freddie Couples (*fig* 9.12), Jim Furyk, Miller Barber, and legions more. It depends on how you're built. Most flying elbows are symptoms of tight chests and shoulder blades, or a *frozen scapula* as it's often called. In other words, people who have thick chests, backs, and shoulders, tend to be more restricted than slender people. As their upper torso rotates in the backswing, if the muscles around the shoulder blades (traps, rhomboids, etc.) are tight, this condition will usually cause the arms to lift and become disconnected from the torso. *To some degree,* this is okay *unless* the arms begin to interrupt the natural rotation of your torso and then disconnect. This lifting also tends to unload your hips as they become destabilized by straightening the leg, overturning, or sliding.

One thing you don't want to do in the golf swing is lose your lower-body stability. However, if you maintain the stability in your lower body and your arms and elbows don't compromise your torso function, let your elbow go where it wants to. Allowing the spine and thorax to rotate easily and without interruption is absolutely crucial, so as long as your trunk is in control, let your elbows do what they want to do.

9.12. A flying right elbow certainly hasn't hindered Freddie Couples.

Regarding the forward swing, one place where you don't want your elbows to fly is right after impact in the chicken wing, where the left arm doesn't refold and swing into a full finish. A chicken wing means that the torso didn't release properly, the arms didn't release properly, and the wrists didn't release properly, in sequence.

In the case of chicken wings, or disconnection of the arms and elbows through the ball, I do recommend putting a head cover, handkerchief, or towel, under the left armpit, and practice rotating the torso through the ball with the upper left arm tucked to the side. Another option is to tie a strap around the torso and upper left arm but let the right arm go where it wants. This will create some extra width with your right arm on the backswing yet keep your elbows from separating through the shot. To make this clear, I don't like straps or props on the right arm during the backswing, but I do recommend them on the left arm for the forward swing. Remember though, these drills should come after or with your flexibility protocol.

# 10

# The Flexibility Programs
## "Just Stretching" Won't Make You Flexible

O ne of the great myths that I've discovered is that the majority of people think that stretching makes you flexible. **I can assure you that "just" stretching won't make you flexible**. Over many years, I have seen virtually thousands of people perform their stretching routines, and seldom have I seen these people actually become flexible! That was certainly true in my case. For years I stretched all the time, and not only did I not achieve superb flexibility, but I actually ended up injuring myself in the process.

I know now, that I'm not alone in this because, for many years, my staff and I have asked virtually thousands of students who have come to our golf schools if they stretched, and the vast majority of them have told us that they do. Yet, seldom have

### There is a right way to stretch and a wrong way to stretch.

we seen very many flexible people! This tells me that there is something wrong with this axiom because, if people stretch properly, they will increase the range of motion in their muscles, enhance the oxygenation of their bodies, rehabilitate injuries, and even prevent injuries from happening in the first place. As mentioned, the vast majority of people that I talk to don't receive these benefits. By deduction, it means that most people are stretching incorrectly. I have learned there is a right way to stretch and a wrong way to stretch. Let me explain the right way to stretch so that you can reap the many benefits that being flexible has to offer.

Here are three rules that must be followed to achieve these benefits:

**Rule 1: Breathe properly.**

**Rule 2: Work the muscle chains in sequence.**

**Rule 3: Maintain consistency in your practice.**

Most flexibility programs fail because one or more of the rules hasn't been followed.

## RULE 1: BREATHE PROPERLY

When we stretch, we're not just stretching, but we're actually breathing oxygen into the nerve spindles and nerve fibers throughout our muscles and into the *fascia* (a fibrous connective tissue, which envelops, separates, or binds a muscle together). Within the fascia are thousands of nerve spindles and nerve fibers which connect with our nervous system and go into our brain.

As we begin contracting and expanding a muscle, the fascia becomes "pulled apart," so to speak, and as they stretch, the nerve spindles and nerve fibers of the muscle become separated from oxygen. As this happens, the nerves cry out to the brain, and we suddenly feel a burn. The burn is in effect a warning signal, or a cry for help, from the brain saying, "We need more oxygen down here!" If the cries for oxygen are ignored, the muscle can tear. The right way to stretch is to start the process of deep breathing and sending oxygen down into the nerve spindles and nerve fibers. As the oxygen flows into the fascia, the nerves begin to bathe in a sea of oxygen and begin to relax. They then say to the muscle, "It's okay now. You can go ahead and contract and expand a little further." As a result, the muscle increases its range of motion and becomes flexible. If, however, the demand for oxygen isn't met, the muscle will tighten up, a process called the *myotatic stretch reflex*. In order to protect itself, the brain signals an impulse down into the stressed area that will tighten up the muscle, which is exactly what we *don't* want to happen. We want to *relax* the muscles, not tighten them. A flexible muscle is a relaxed muscle—nothing more, nothing less. And, a relaxed muscle is one that has oxygen in it.

Not only does the oxygenating of our muscles stretch that muscle, our entire body receives the benefits of breathing. The diaphragm will help push the oxygen and blood into the heart, the heart then pumps the oxygen and blood throughout the body, and even more importantly, the head will begin to sit right on top of the shoulders. I encourage you to stand up right now and try that. Inhale and exhale deeply, and notice how, on the inhalation, the chest not only expands but pushes your head back on top of your shoulders. When the head sits right on top of the clavicles, gravity is allowed to circulate the oxygen and blood up to nourish the brain. Nearly all people who embark on my flexibility program report back that they begin to feel taller and lighter, and that they focus more clearly. This is from the increase in oxygen and blood to the brain due to the improved posture. Since we're actually doing over 20,000 repetitions of breathing a day, you can see how important breathing is. In time, developing proper breathing patterns will strengthen your body, and emotions, in a number of ways. The body's breathing pattern will begin to sustain itself.

Although there are a lot of different breathing techniques, I've narrowed it down to two methods that I employ in my stretching protocols. I'm going to teach you a breathing method for the static stretches and a method for the active stretches. For the static stretches, we're going to employ the East-West breathing and for the active stretches, we're going to reverse the process.

## STATIC STRETCHES

For static stretches, where we hold the pose, I want you to inhale through the nose, making sure that you expand your lower abdomen in a side-to-side manner. This breathing, called East-West, ensures that we employ intra-abdominal pressure (IAP) into the solar plexus, which will, among other things, help to stabilize the spine. Imagine you have an inner tube fit snugly around your midsection, just under your rib cage. As you inhale, try to expand the entire inner tube *out-ward*. Or, as I like to say, "get fat" by allowing your love handles to go outward. (We men sometimes find ourselves "sucking it in" in an effort to impress the ladies down at muscle beach.) To effectively breathe East-West, I want you to give up your egos and let it out. My experience has shown me that very few people can effectively perform East-West breathing in the beginning.

To test this breathing method, have someone put their fingers on the sides of your abdomen (where your love handles are) and as you breathe in, push out against your helper's fingers on the love handles. I've found that few people can do this very well in the beginning. However, by being conscious of this even while walking around during the day, you'll begin to breathe powerfully and effectively. In time you'll find yourself breathing this way automatically and at that point you'll find that it has a very calming and confident effect in your state of well being.

Although the upper chest will also expand, the emphasis and focus should be on the lower abdomen. A huge mistake in people's breathing occurs when they just breathe with the upper chest in a "panting" manner, which is, in fact, actually a form of holding the breath.

At the end of the inhalation I want you to actually feel a tightening up, or a pushing out, at your sides until they're firm. This is important to attain the "contract-relax" response that we want. Only tighten your sides at the end of the inhalation, not before. In certain postures this will be easier to do and more difficult in others. After you've held your breath for a moment, exhale out through your mouth, making sure that you completely empty your entire solar plexus. The breath should sound like a "Ha-a-a-a-h" and should be relatively loud. This point is crucial in the process because it is at this point where the total relaxation occurs. You'll notice that as you're exhaling you'll immediately go deeper and deeper into the stretch. This contract-relax process is very powerful and is sure to enhance your overall breathing capacity.

The main point here is to make sure that your inhalation and exhalation patterns are full and deep. In other words, don't cut off the inhalation or exhalation until you've reached the end of the breaths. You'll probably notice that if you try to force a stretch, you won't be able to sustain your breathing pattern and will instead be forced to hold your breath. If this happens, it is simply a sign that you're going too far at this point in the stretch. Be patient and allow the breathing patterns to take you deeper into the stretch.

Let's review: (1) You want to inhale through the nose, making sure that you're pushing the sides of your lower abdomen outward (at the love handles) until they're firm; (2) at the end of the inhalation, hold for a moment; and (3) exhale *completely* forcing *all* of the breath out of the lower abdomen. Pause, and then repeat.

## ACTIVE STRETCHES

On active stretches, the breathing pattern is the opposite of the static stretches. In this case, we're going to exhale *out* through the mouth on the first phase, and then inhale *in* through the nose on the release. In addition, we're only going to hold the stretch for one to two seconds. Nearly everybody I train has trouble coordinating this at first, so I tell them to think of baseball. Think of the first out. Breathe *out* on the first move, and *inhale* on the release.

Holding the pose for only one to two seconds prevents any chance of a myotactic stretch reflex to occur. This is a tightening of the muscle, in essence shutting it down. Because you're only holding the stretch such a short time, there's no chance of any excess tightening of the muscle. Active stretches will also, in time, strengthen the fast twitch fibers of the muscle.

There is much controversy about whether active stretches or static stretches are better for you. Advocates for active stretches say that static stretches and breathing slow down the fast twitch fibers in the muscle, which make

---

you slower and increase the wear and tear of the fascia because you're holding the muscle for a long time, day after day, month after month, year after year. This is very common in ballet dancers, who hold poses in awkward positions for years, and commonly end up with a multitude of serious injuries.

I have found, however, that for muscle rehabilitation and improving one's posture, a static stretch is superior to an active stretch because the muscle fibers have more time to receive oxygen while they're in proper position and therefore the brain can now "remember" the proper neuron pattern. An active stretch is superior for sports where we're trying to improve speed and quickness, such as running and jumping.

In my programs, I use the best of both worlds and employ both methods.

## RULE 2: WORK THE MUSCLE CHAINS IN SEQUENCE

Muscles work in chains. Much like tile on a roof, although they're all individual, they all work in unison and synergize with one another. There are several chains of muscles in our bodies, but the ones that we're going

*Isolating and stretching individual muscles without stretching out the other muscles in the chain is probably the No. 1 mistake the average person makes in their stretching.*

to be concerned with here are the posterior chain (the muscles on our back side that run from our heels up to our necks), and the anterior chain (three major muscles on the front of our hips that intertwine with the diaphragm). The muscles in these chains that have the most influence are called *polyarticular* (muscles that cross over two joints) and are on the same side of the body. When one muscle in the chain is shortened, the entire chain is affected, in effect shortening the rest of the chain with it.

For example, the calf muscle in the posterior chain works in unison with the hamstrings, glutes, trapezius, etc. If, for example, a person has a tight calf, almost invariably, we'll see a tight back or shoulder. Therefore, if I want to stretch out my back, I'll definitely need to stretch out the rest of the muscles in that chain, i.e., calves, hamstrings, glutes, etc. If I only stretched the shoulders, and the other muscles in the chain are tight or dysfunctional, they will in time get pulled back by the other tight muscles in that chain. Simply isolating and stretching just one aspect of the chain will not make for permanent results.

Isolating and stretching individual muscles without stretching out the other muscles in the chain is probably the No. 1 mistake (along with improper breathing) the average person makes in their stretching.

It's important to work the muscle chains in order, from the ground up. Don't worry—you won't need to learn all of the muscle chains. The programs in this book are arranged for the muscles to be stretched in order, and in their respective chains. If you do the stretches in sequence, you'll be working the proper muscle chains in the proper order.

## RULE 3: MAINTAINING CONSISTENCY

Consistency is extremely important. I stress this because our sedentary sitting-down lifestyle tightens us up to some degree every day. Every day that we sit down we're "exercising" our hips in a flexion position, and therefore I feel that we must all incorporate a proper flexibility program into our daily lives to counterbalance the damaging effects of this lifestyle. Since most golfers, and especially our senior players, have tightened up as a result of this lifestyle, the majority of them must "build up" so to speak, to attain a flexible and functional body. It's better to be consistent and do a little bit every day, than it is to do a lot two or three days a week. But don't shortchange yourself. If you're not making the strides that you're hoping for, you're probably not doing enough. Also, the more that you do in the beginning, the faster you'll attain results.

In the beginning, most of you aren't in a position to just do it once in a while. Think of these programs as if you were going to train for a marathon. If you just went for a jog every few days, there's no way that you'd develop the

*The more flexibility you attain, the more you can maintain.*

endurance necessary to finish 26.2 miles. By working your programs on a consistent basis and then resting occasionally, you'll eventually "build up enough endurance to finish the race" and achieve superb flexibility. That's the best way to approach flexibility training.

I'm sure you're thinking "Oh no, I've got to do this forever." Don't fret because I have some good news. *The more flexibility you attain, the more you can maintain.* In other words, you won't have to do as much because, the more you train your body to breathe throughout your muscle chains, the more your body learns how to breathe on its own. Subsequently, your daily flexibility program certainly won't take very long. I've been stretching properly for over 25 years, and my daily program now takes me around 10 minutes. When I started, however, it took me around 20 to 40 minutes. I assure you, it's been well worth it.

My goal with my clients is to get them to incorporate their flex programs into their daily lives, just like brushing your teeth. I highly recommend that you do your program five or six days a week, always taking one day off allowing your body to completely rest.

Don't rush into the program and burn out either. Remember the tortoise won the race, not the hare.

## WHEN TO STRETCH

Anytime is a good time to stretch, but the morning is best because you're preparing the muscles for all the activity you're going to encumber during the day. Doing short stretches throughout the day (especially the psoas stretch) is also beneficial for restoring range of motion and energy in your body. If you want to do some stretches at night, go right ahead.

## WARM UP BEFORE STRETCHING

It's a good idea to warm up before you stretch. You can do a little running in place, swinging the power swing fan or any other cardio exercise for a few minutes. Heat in the body is what we're striving for, so a little warm up is good. You'll find too that the deeper and longer you breathe, the more you'll heat up and perspire. On the Long Program, a warmup is not that crucial because the active stretches themselves warm you up.

## WARM UP BEFORE OTHER EXERCISE PROGRAMS

You should always stretch before any exercise program. Ideally, do the entire stretch program. However, if you're short on time, then the Pre-golf Warmup will suffice. You can do the Post-golf Cooldown when you're finished, or the relaxation poses.

## HYDRATION

Drink fresh water (not tap water) before, during, and after your workout. This will help your oxygen and blood circulation as you work through your program.

## THE PROGRAMS

There are three basic programs: the Short Program for beginners, the Intermediate Program, and the Advanced Program. I've also included the Pre-golf Warm-up, as well as the Post-golf Cooldown, which are important as the muscles should be warmed before we play and unwound after play.

The Short Program and Intermediate Program incorporate passive or static stretches, where you'll hold the poses for 20 to 40 seconds. These poses are designed to synchronize the muscle chains, increase oxygenation in your body, and help restore better posture.

The Advanced Program incorporates an active stretch program, where you only hold each pose for one to two seconds. This program is most beneficial for people who want to do more active forms of exercises, such as cardio training, basketball, tennis, etc., and yes, you can use it before you play golf, too.

## RELAXATION POSES

I cannot stress relaxation poses enough! You should do them as much as possible. The Supine Groin stretch (S49, p.199) is the most effective pose that I've ever seen in taming the powerful hip flexors, especially the iliopsoas. Relaxing the psoas is critical because it's connected to the diaphragm. Every breath you take involves the hip flexor, and every step you take involves the hip flexor and diaphragm. I highly recommend that you take one or two days off a week and just do the Supine Groin stretch, even up to an hour or more if you can. This was the pose that convinced me of the importance of flexibility training and changed my life. Many people feel that the Supine Groin isn't doing anything while they're in the pose, but I assure you it is. Relaxing the hips is absolutely crucial in developing anatomical function. Once the hip flexor is relaxed, every muscle in the body can function properly.

## MIXING UP YOUR PROGRAMS

Mix up the programs. After all, doing the same program every day can get monotonous and cause you to burn out from boredom. After you master the programs, combine different parts of the different programs into one.

*The main thing to remember if you mix up your stretch programs is to always start from the ground up and always stretch the lower body first.*

For example, let's say you do the Short Program lower body stretches, but you want to get more aggressive with the spinal twists. Go ahead and do the upper body stretches in the Long Program. Or, you can do the active stretches for the lower body first, and then do some static stretches for the upper body next.

The main thing to remember if you mix up your stretch programs is to always start from the ground up and *always stretch the lower body first.* In other words, don't start with the upper body, especially the spinal twists.

In an effort to get more flexible in their upper trunk so they can get a bigger shoulder turn, many people start right off on their spinal twists, and don't do anything else. If you want more shoulder turn, loosen up the hips more! I've seen a lot of people increase their shoulder turns up to 40 degrees just by loosening their hips. In most cases, an inflexible muscle group can be loosened up just by stretching the other end of that muscle chain.

## INJURIES

The programs in this book were not designed to treat specific injuries. They were designed to increase the range of motion in a person's body to create a freer and more powerful golf swing. I am continually asked if this program will help this or that condition, and I normally reply that proper flexibility programs can help nearly all conditions—*if* the stretches are done and conducted in the proper sequence. However, all stretching protocols must be designed for that specific injury. If you have an injury, first see a licensed physician or anatomical functionalist before you go any further.

If you feel some pain when doing a stretch, stop that stretch immediately but continue to do the other stretches in the order prescribed.

Now that you know the rules, let's get into the programs.

# SHORT PROGRAM

1. OVERHEAD
EXTENSION
(S36, page 188)

2. COUNTER
(S23, page 179)

3. CATS & DOGS
(S24, page 180)

4. DOWNWARD DOG
(S1, page 165)

5. PSOAS
(S15, page 173)

**-OR-**

STANDING PSOAS
(S15A, page 173)

6. SPREAD-FOOT
FORWARD BEND
(S2, page 165)

7. RUNNERS
(S3, page 166)

8. SITTING WALL
(S17, page 174)

9. BRIDGE
(S25, page 180)

10. PRETZEL
(S32, page 185)

*Secrets of Golf Instruction and Flexibility*

11. CROCODILE
(S34, page 187)

12. CATS & DOGS
(S24, page 180)

13. PECTORALIS
(S37, page 189)

14. ARM CIRCLES
(S38, page 190)

15. ELBOW CURLS
(S39, page 191)

*Note: A detailed explanation for each of the stretches in these programs can be found in Chapter 11. Each stretch has a corresponding reference number as well as page number to assist in finding the detailed explanation if necessary.*

# INTERMEDIATE PROGRAM

1. OVERHEAD
EXTENSION
(S36, page 188)

2. COUNTER
(S23, page 179)

3. CATS & DOGS
(S24, page 180)

4. COBRA
(S26, page 181)

5. DOWNWARD DOG
(S1, page 165)

6. PLANK
(S45, page 196)

7. PSOAS
(S15, page 173)

8. TRIANGLE
(S27, page 181)

9. EXTENDED
LATERAL
(S28, page 182)

10. SPREAD-FOOT
FORWARD BEND
(S2, page 165)

11. RUNNERS
(S3, page 166)

12. SOLO SITTING
WALL
(S18, page 175)

**13. HIP-THIGH EXTENSIONS (S19, page 176)**

**14. HIP CROSSOVERS (S20, page 177)**

**15. PRETZEL (S32, page 185)**

**16. UPPER SPINAL FLOOR TWIST (S33, page 186)**

-OR-

**17. EXTENDED HALF BOW (S29A, page 183)**

**THE BOW (S29, page 183)**

**18. WHY ME'S (S40, page 192)**

**19. BREAST STROKE (S41, page 193)**

**20. ARM CIRCLES (S38, page 190)**

**21. ELBOW CURLS (S39, page 191)**

**22. AIR BENCH (S4, page 166)**

**23. STATIC BACK PRESS (S48, page 199)**

# ADVANCED PROGRAM

1. SINGLE-LEG PELVIC
TILT
(S5, page 167)

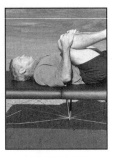

2. DOUBLE-LEG
PELVIC TILT
(S6, page 167)

3. BENT-KNEE
HAMSTRING
(S7, page 168)

4. STRAIGHT-LEG
HAMSTRING
(S9, page 169)

5. ADDUCTOR
(S10, page 169)

6. ABDUCTOR
(S11, page 170)

7. QUADRICEPS
(S12, page 171)

-OR-

8. PSOAS
(S15, page 173)

STANDING PSOAS
(S15A, page 173)

9. SOLO SITTING
WALL
(S18, page 175)

10. HIP-THIGH
EXTENSIONS)
(S19, page 176)

**11. INT. & EXT. HIP ROTATORS**
(S21, page 178)

**12. SEATED FORWARD BEND**
(S30, page 184)

**13. RUSSIAN BALL TWIST (OR 15)**
(S35, page 188)

**-OR-**

**PRETZEL**
(S32, page 185)

**14. LOCUST**
(S47, page 198)

**-OR-**

**EXTENDED LOCUST**
(S47B, page 198)

**15. LATERAL BALL ROLLS**
(S42, page 193)

**16. FROG**
(S22, page 178)

**17. INT. & EXT. SHOULDER ROTATORS (S43, pg 194)**

**18. WHY ME'S**
(S40, page 192)

**19. BREAST STROKE**
(S41, page 193)

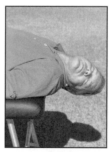

**20. HEAD & NECK**
(S44, page 195)

**21. WALL SQUATS**
(S46, page 197)

*The Flexibility Programs*

# PRE-GOLF WARM-UP

**1. OVERHEAD EXTENSION**
(S36, page 188)

**2. COUNTER**
(S23, page 179)

**3. CATS & DOGS**
(S24, page 180)

**4. DOWNWARD DOG**
(S1, page 165)

**5. PSOAS**
(S15, page 173)

**6. RUNNERS**
(S3, page 166)

**7. PRETZEL**
(S32, page 185)

**8. ARM CIRCLES**
(S38, page 190)

**9. ELBOW CURLS**
(S39, page 191)

# POST-GOLF COOLDOWN

1. OVERHEAD
EXTENSION
(S36, page 188)

2. COUNTER
(S23, page 179)

3. CATS & DOGS
(S24, page 180)

4. DOWNWARD DOG
(S1, page 165)

5. CROCODILE
(S34, page 187)

6. CATS & DOGS
(S24, page 180)

7. STATIC BACK
PRESS
(S48, page 199)

# RELAXATION POSES

1. CATS & DOGS
(S24, page 180)

2. DOWNWARD DOG
(S1, page 165)

3. STATIC BACK
PRESS
(S48, page 199)

4. SUPINE GROIN
(S49, page 199)

# *Flexibility Stretches*

## LOWER BODY STRETCHES: LEGS

11.1. Body shaped like a "V".

### S1. Downward Dog

**Benefit**: This outstanding whole-body stretch affects the entire posterior muscle chain and helps strengthen the legs, hips, and shoulders. This pose is a must.

**Directions:** Start on the floor on all fours, raise your hips, and straighten your legs. Focus on pushing your knees out through the backs of your legs, while pressing your heels towards the floor. At the same time, raise your tailbone to the sky. Pressing into the ground with your hands, try to get your body shaped like a "V" (*fig* 11.1) and remember to *breathe*. Hold this pose for 30 seconds.

## S2. Spread-Foot Forward Bend

**Benefit**: This wonderful stretch for the adductors, inner thighs, hamstrings, and lower back, results in a greater rotation of the hips, and allows the forward leg to separate from the trailing leg during the forward swing.

**Directions:** Spread your feet wide and keep your legs tight while bending forward, placing your hands on the floor (*fig* 11.2). If you can't reach the floor without bending your knees, use a prop. Breathe deeply for 20 to 30 seconds.

11.2. Whether you use a prop or not, keep your legs tight.

11.3. Place both hands on top of chair.

11.4. Walk your hands down the chair, keeping your front knee straight.

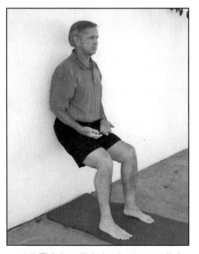

11.5. Thighs slightly above parallel to the floor.

## S3. Runners Stretch

**Benefit**: This stretches the hamstrings and calves. Hamstring flexibility contributes to mobilization and stabilization of the hips and helps keep the knees flexed and loaded.

**Directions: Step 1**. Start by kneeling on the floor and put both hands on the top of a chair (*fig* 11.3). Place your right foot forward, pointing straight ahead. Bring the left knee flush up against the right heel. (If you have knee problems and it is difficult for you to get down on the floor, you may start from a standing position, making sure that both feet are in line with each other.)

**Step 2**. Slowly, stand up, straightening both knees, especially the front knee, and make sure the rear foot is flat on the ground.

**Step 3**. Begin "walking" your hands down the chair, attempting to get your fingertips to the floor (*fig* 11.4). However, do *not* let the front knee bend. When you feel the back of your front knee begin to burn, back off slightly and breathe deeper. It's not how far down to the floor you get that counts, but rather how deeply you breathe into the stretch. You'll notice that, as you breathe, you will drop a little more. Don't force this stretch, but rather breathe into it. Hold for 30 to 60 seconds, and repeat on the other side.

## S4. Air Bench

**Benefit**: This exercise strengthens your legs, which will help stabilize your lower body as well as help tame the powerful hip flexors.

*Secrets of Golf Instruction and Flexibility*

**Directions:** Sit against a wall with the small of your back pressing against the wall. Keep your thighs slightly above parallel to the floor at about a 100- to 110-degree angle (*fig* 11.5). Your knees should be directly above your heels. Make sure that your shoulder, hips, knees, and feet are in alignment, with your feet pointing straight ahead. If this is hard on your knees, modify the pose by not squatting as much to relieve the pressure. Stay in this pose for two minutes.

## S5. Single-Leg Pelvic Tilt

**Benefit**: This active stretch warms up the lower-back muscles and prepares the back for other stretches. In the golf swing, this stretch allows the lower back to flex forward more easily in the stance.

**Directions:** Lie on your back with your legs straight. Bend your exercising leg. Place one hand behind your knee, and the other on your knee-cap. Using your abdominals, pull your knee back toward your armpit as you exhale (*fig* 11.6). Hold for one to two seconds, release, and inhale. Switch and do the other side. Do 5 to 10 repetitions.

11.6. Knee pulled back.

## S6. Double-Leg Pelvic Tilt

**Benefit**: This stretch warms up both sides simultaneously.

**Directions:** Lie on your back as directed in the Single-Leg Pelvic Tilt (S5). This time, take hold of both knees and pull them back toward your armpits as you exhale (*fig* 11.7). Hold for one to two seconds, release, and inhale. Do 5 to 10 repetitions.

11.7. Both knees pulled back.

11.8. Rope placed around bottom of right foot.

11.9. Leg pointing toward ceiling.

11.10. Keep your legs straight and lower back pressed down.

## S7. Bent-Knee Hamstring

**Benefit**: This stretches out the lower hamstring muscle just above and behind the knee. Keeping the lower hamstring flexible allows the knee and pelvis to remain stable and flexed throughout the golf swing. Inflexible hamstrings make it difficult for any golfer to keep the knees flexed and stay down into the shot. The Bent-Knee Hamstring is a preparatory stretch for the Straight-Leg Hamstring (S9).

**Directions:** You'll need a rope for this stretch. Lie on your back and bend your right knee. Raise your right leg so that your thigh is vertical to the ground and your lower leg is horizontal to the ground. Place your left hand on your lower right thigh just above your knee to stabilize your leg. Holding a rope in your right hand, place the rope around the bottom of your right foot (*fig* 11.8). Begin exhaling, contract your right quad, and raise your lower leg so that it's pointing toward the ceiling (*fig* 11.9). Make sure your foot is always pulled back. Apply some pressure at the end of the stretch, holding for one to two seconds. Don't lift your pelvis off of the floor and don't force the stretch. If your flexibility won't allow you to get your leg vertical to the floor, you may have to lower your thigh slightly in the starting position.

Perform 5 to 10 repetitions and repeat on the other side.

## S8. Supine Leg Chain

**Benefit:** This is a great exercise for stretching all of the muscles in the posterior muscle chain from the glutes on down to your calves.

**Directions:** You'll need a rope for this stretch. Lie on your back with both of your legs extended. Wrap the rope around the balls of your feet and make sure your feet are pulled back toward you. Gently lift your legs up as far as you can *without your knees bending* while keeping your lower back pressed to the floor (*fig* 11.10). As you're pulling the feet and legs toward you with the rope, you should be simultaneously pushing your legs away from you, creating isometric/eccentric contraction.

## S9. Straight-Leg Hamstring

**Benefit**: This stretches out the main belly of the hamstring. A functional hamstring allows for the stability of the pelvis and maintaining flex in the knees throughout the swing. Tight hamstrings often result in the straightening of the legs and a loss of mobility and stability during the swing.

11.11. Foot arched with leg up.

**Directions:** You'll need a rope for this stretch. Lie on your back with your legs straight. Place the rope around the ball of your right foot. Arch your foot back and lift your leg up (*fig* 11.11), always keeping your *knees locked*. If you feel pressure in your lower back, bend the opposite knee for relief. At the end of the stretch, give a gentle tug on the rope and hold for one to two seconds. Repeat 5 to 10 times on both sides.

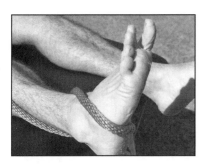
11.12. Rope placement.

## S10. Adductor Stretch

**Benefit**: This stretch allows the inner thighs to remain flexible, which will free up the pelvis and allow it to rotate to maximum capacity. This will also allow the left leg to separate from the right on the downswing.

---

11.13. Leg extended to the side.

**Directions:** You'll need a rope for this stretch. Lie on your back with both legs extended and your feet pigeon-toed. Place the rope around the right foot, then wrap it to the inside of the right leg and then back around to the outside of the leg (*fig* 11.12). Hold the rope with the opposite (left) hand. Keep the leg straight (and the foot still pigeon-toed), and gently extend the leg out to the side as far as you can *without* straining (*fig* 11.13). Give a gentle tug at the end of the stretch and hold for one to two seconds. Repeat and do the other side. For a full workout, do 5 to 10 repetitions on both sides.

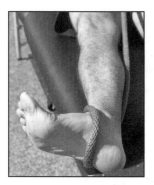
11.14. Rope placement.

## S11. Abductor Stretch

**Benefit:** This exercise stretches the outer thighs and hips, allowing the lower body to stabilize throughout the swing. Tight hips slow down the centrifugal force created during the golf swing.

**Directions:** You'll need a rope for this stretch. Lie on your back with both legs extended and your feet flared, both facing in the same direction. Both feet should be facing away from the direction you are going to stretch (i.e., if you are stretching your right leg to the left, both feet should face right). Place the rope around the right foot, and wrap it to the outside of the right leg and then back around to the inside of the leg (*fig* 11.14). Hold the rope with the right (same-side) hand. Keeping the leg relatively straight and the foot still flared out, gently extend the leg across your body as far as you can *without* straining (*fig* 11.15). Use the opposite hand to gently tug at the end of the stretch and hold for one to two seconds. Try not to raise the leg too high. You'll feel

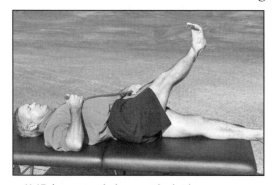
11.15. Leg extended across the body.

*Secrets of Golf Instruction and Flexibility*

this in the outside of the upper thigh. Repeat and do the other side. For a full workout, do 5 to 10 repetitions on both sides.

## S12. Quadriceps Stretch

**Benefit**: This stretch loosens up the quadriceps muscles, which are too tight in most people. This stretch allows the knees, legs, and hips to synchronize and work together.

11.16. Pull the foot back to the buttocks. Don't allow the thigh to go forward.

**Directions:** You'll need a rope for this stretch. Double loop a rope around your lower leg. Lie on your side with your thigh in line with your torso. Pull the foot back to your buttocks and hold for one to two seconds (*fig* 11.16). Release back to the starting position. Make sure that you don't allow your thigh to go forward of your torso. Repeat 5 to 10 times on each side.

11.17. Foot behind buttocks.

## Alternate (S12A): Standing Quadriceps Stretch

**Directions:** Standing with your thigh in line with your torso, grab your foot. Bring it up toward your buttocks (*fig* 11.17). Try not to lean forward. Hold for one to two seconds and release. You may do this stretch statically if you choose.

Active stretch: 5 to 10 times each leg

Static stretch: 20 seconds each side

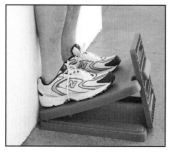

11.18. Stand on a slant board and continually squeeze and release glutes.

11.19. Place heels against wall.

## LOWER BODY STRETCHES: HIPS

## S13. The Standing Drop-Off (with Gluteal Contractions)

**Benefit:** This is a powerful pose that will help restore the ankle, knee, hip, and shoulder relationship. In addition, it will help release your hips and at the same time strengthen your glutes and put them in a neutral position, which will, in turn, allow your shoulders to come back into proper position. This pose is a must for people who want to improve their posture.

**Directions:** Stand on a slant board (plank of wood is fine) or a foot stool (or other object) against a wall with your heels below your toes (*fig* 11.18). Make sure that your heels are against the wall (*fig* 11.19). It is important to have your feet pointing straight ahead and directly in line with your hips and shoulders. Although we want the feet to be angled upward, there should be no discomfort in the pose. Let your body relax. Now, begin to gently but firmly contract (squeeze) your glutes (your fanny). Hold for one second and release. Continue to contract them for the entire duration of the exercise.

When you're finished with the pose and you step off the prop, you'll be amazed at the "lifting" of the upper thorax and the improved posture that you'll suddenly attain.

You can stay in this pose up to 10 minutes for therapy, and eventually cut it down to 2 to 4 minutes. (This pose is one of my personal favorites and I do it every day.)

## S14. Active Groin Stretch

**Benefit:** This is a great pose that uses gravity to relax and loosen the powerful hip flexors. Relaxing the hips is crucial in developing superb flexibility.

**Directions:** Lie on a table, making sure that your tailbone is off the edge and pushing into the end of the table. Clasp your hands and place them under the back of your right knee. Make sure that your right thigh is perpendicular to the table (*fig* 11.20). There should be a small arch in your back. Relax your extended (left) leg completely and also relax your upper body. Hold for one minute and switch to the other leg. You'll notice that your extended leg will begin to relax completely. If you want to stay in the stretch longer, by all means do so.

11.20. Lie at the end of a table and relax hips and shoulders.

## S15. Psoas Stretch

**Benefit:** This stretch is a must for the hips.

**Directions:** Kneel on the ground with your feet, knees, hips and shoulders all in a straight line. Place the forward foot approximately one and one-half to two feet in front of the knee. Keep your spine vertical and sink down toward the floor as you lift your chest (*fig* 11.21). You should feel this deep in your groin. If your stability is good, you can raise your arms over your head or even place a golf club behind your back for increased extension. Hold this pose for 20 to 30 seconds on static stretches and do 5 to 10 repetitions for active stretches then switch and do the other side.

11.21. Kneeling psoas stretch.

## Alternate (S15A): Standing Psoas

I recommend that most people do this stretch in a standing position several times a day to counter the effects of our sedentary lifestyle (*fig* 11.22).

11.22. Standing psoas stretch.

---

*Flexibility Stretches*

11.23. Keep your torso as straight as possible.

## S16. Warrior II

**Benefit:** This pose develops strength and flexibility in the legs and also brings elasticity to the back muscles.

**Directions:** Stand at attention. Then spread your feet approximately 4 feet apart. Keep your right foot straight ahead and turn your left foot outward 90 degrees. The ankles should be in a direct line with one another. Exhale and bend the left knee so that the thigh is parallel to the floor. (If you can't go down that low, don't worry about it—just do the best you can.) The bent knee should not extend beyond the ankle but should be in line with the ankle. Keep the rear leg straight. Stretch out your arms and hand sideways as though two people were pulling you from each end (*fig* 11.23). Your chest should be facing the direction that you started, but your head should be looking out over your extended arm. Hold for 20 to 30 seconds. Switch and do the other side.

11.24. Legs straight, feet arched back.

## S17. Sitting Wall

**Benefit**: This great hamstring and glute stretch sets the pelvis, which aids in attaining better posture and stabilizing the hips in the address position, as well as maintaining a proper spine angle throughout the swing.

**Directions:** Sit against a wall "at attention." Press your shoulders into the wall and make sure that your tailbone is as close to the wall as possible. In the beginning, if it's too uncomfortable to get your tailbone close to the wall, back off until it's manageable. In time this will become easier to do. As you press your shoulders back, make sure that you are lifting your sternum as you breathe deeply and fully with your abdomen, making sure you push your abdomen outward on the inhalation. Pull your feet back while pressing your knees to the floor (*fig* 11.24). Also, try to keep your chin level and your head against the wall. Many people won't be able to get their head back against the wall while keeping their chin level, but do the best you can. This pose is very difficult for many people, so don't force it. Pay attention and *breathe*. Hold for one to two minutes. For a more advanced pose, try to keep your heels off of the floor.

## S18. Solo Sitting Wall

**Benefit**: This powerful pose not only stretches the hamstrings but also helps lengthen the anterior muscle chain (the iliacus, psoas, and diaphragm), whose dysfunction is epidemic in our digital world. The benefits of this pose extend far beyond the musculoskeltal world and will help create better health and fitness because of the improved function of the diaphragm.

11.25. Half foam roller behind shoulder blades.

**Directions:** You'll need a one-half foam roller and a rope for this stretch. Sit against a wall "at attention." Take a one-half foam roller (or a 6- to 8-inch-diameter towel), and place it behind your back near the bottom of your shoulder blades (*fig* 11.25). Press your shoulders into the foam roller as if you were trying to get your shoulders to touch the wall. At the same time try to get the back of your head to touch the wall, but don't let your head arch backwards. Keep your jaw line level, even if you can't get your head to touch the wall.

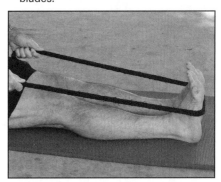

11.26. Use a rope to pull back feet.

Now breathe *deeply* while lifting your sternum and expanding your abdomen. For a more advanced stretch, wrap a rope around the soles of your feet, and pull your feet back toward you while pushing your knees to the floor (*fig* 11.26). For many people, this is very uncomfortable in the beginning, so be sure not to force the pose.

Your primary focus should be on pressing your shoulders back toward the wall and breathing deeply. The secondary focus should be on pulling the feet back and the knees toward the floor. Many people bend forward while they pull the feet back, which is counterproductive. Hold this pose for two to four minutes in the beginning, and as you get more proficient, you can cut down the time to one to two minutes.

## S19. Hip-Thigh Extensions

In addition to flexibility, we must also have a good balance of strength in the muscle groups, which will allow the body to achieve stability. This is especially true in the posterior muscles, and especially the glutes. Due to the forward-bending flexion culture we live in, the muscles of our anterior (front muscles) get too tight and pull the torso forward, thus weakening and tightening the posterior (rear muscles). As a result, our back muscles generally become weaker, thus preventing the necessary stability that is so crucial for our golf swings.

**Benefit**: These extensions are terrific for strengthening back-side muscles while stretching the front side.

**Directions:** Lying supine on the floor, bend your left knee and straighten your right leg (*fig* 11.27). Your palms should be face up at 45 degrees from your body. Now lift your entire body up one to two inches by pushing off your left foot (*fig* 11.28). This is the start position. Continue to lift your entire body in a straight line so that your thighs are parallel

11.27. Left knee bent with straight right leg.

11.28. Lift with your torso, not just your leg.

11.29. Body in a straight line with thighs parallel.

*Secrets of Golf Instruction and Flexibility*

to each other (*fig* 11.29). The only parts of your body that are in contact with the floor are your arms, upper back, and left foot. Remember that, when you lift, you're lifting primarily with your torso, not just the leg. The extended leg just goes along for the ride.

Hold for three seconds and lower yourself back down to one inch off the floor. Pause and repeat 5 to 10 times. Be sure to keep the hips in a straight line. Repeat on the other side and eventually build up your repetitions.

## S20. Hip Crossovers

**Benefit**: This is an excellent exercise for creating bilateral mobility in both hips, which also aids in developing a greater shoulder turn.

**Directions:** Lie on the floor with both knees bent, your feet flat on the floor, and your arms out to your sides. Cross your right ankle over your left knee and slightly press your right knee away from you (*fig* 11.30). Now roll your right knee and foot over to the left so that your right foot is firmly on the floor (*fig* 11.31). Don't force this stretch. As you roll over, make sure that you apply slight pressure on the knee (pushing it forward), while you look in the opposite direction with your head. Hold this pose for one minute, then switch and do the other side.

11.30. Right ankle over left knee.

11.31. Right knee foot over left, firmly on the floor.

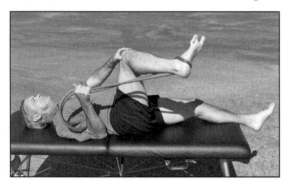
11.32. Thigh is perpendicular to the floor and lower leg 90 degrees to the thigh.

# S21. Internal & External Hip Rotators

**Benefit**: This stretch will help open your powerful deep six rotators in the hips, which allow the lateral rotation of the thigh. This will allow the hips to turn in an unrestricted manner in the golf swing.

**Directions:** You'll need a rope for this stretch. Lie on your back with your knees bent. Bend your right knee and place the rope under your right foot and wrap it to the inside of your lower leg and then back to the outside. Hold the rope in your right hand. Your thigh should be 90 degrees to the floor and 90 degrees to your lower leg (*fig* 11.32). Place your left hand on your right thigh just above the knee for stability. Now slowly rotate your calf and foot outward (*fig* 11.33), making sure that your right thigh remains perpendicular to the ground. Hold for one to two seconds and repeat 5 to 10 times.

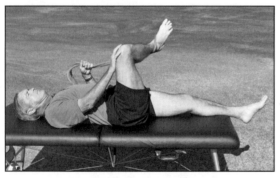
11.33. Rotate calf outward.

After finishing the outward (external) movements, turn the lower calf inward (*fig* 11.34) and repeat 5 to 10 times. Repeat with the other leg.

# S22. Frog

**Benefit**: This stretch will allow your inner thighs to stretch and help release the hips, relaxing the adductors and help free up the pelvis.

11.34. Rotate calf inward.

**Directions:** Lie on your back and bring your feet up toward your torso. Bring the soles of your feet together, allowing your knees to turn out (*fig* 11.35).

11.35. Soles of feet together with knees turned out.

11.36. Lift pelvis off the ground keeping knees open.

Do not force your knees down, but allow your thighs to gently relax into a comfortable position. Hold for one to two minutes.

## Alternate (S22A): Elevated Frog (Advanced)

**Benefit**: This is a more advanced stretch that will help strengthen the glutes as you stretch your hip flexors. This also helps tame the nerves in the sympathetic nervous system located in your solar plexus.

**Directions:** Lift your pelvis well off the ground, making sure to keep your knees open and relaxed (*fig* 11.36). It doesn't matter where you place your arms. They can be above your head, next to your body, or on your belly. Simply find the most comfortable position for them. Hold for one to two minutes.

## LOWER BODY & UPPER TRUNK

## S23. Counter Stretch

**Benefit**: This stretches the hamstrings, glutes, and shoulders, allowing you to stabilize and maintain a proper hip tilt throughout the swing.

**Directions:** From the Overhead Extension stretch (S36, p. 188), lean forward and place your hands against a wall. Keeping the weight on the balls of your feet,

11.37. Push your hands into the wall, extending your torso.

11.38. Arched back (cat).

11.39. Back down (dog).

push your hands into the wall, extending your torso with your legs tight (*fig* 11.37). Hold for 20 seconds.

## S24. Cats & Dogs

**Benefit**: This excellent stretch for the hips, back, chest, and spine helps the hips and shoulders work together and increases range of motion of the pelvis and spine throughout the swing.

**Directions:** Start on the floor in an all-fours position, with your hands under your shoulders and your knees under your hips. Breathe *out* as you arch your back up (like a scared cat) while looking at your navel (*fig* 11.38). Then breathe *in* as you slowly arch your back down while looking up at the sky (like a happy dog [*fig* 11.39]). Don't rock back and forth. Hold each position for one to two seconds. Repeat five to eight times.

11.40. Hips raised.

## S25. Bridge

**Benefit**: This stretches the abdominals and hip flexors and strengthens the glutes and lower back. It increases range of motion in the trunk and adds stability and power to the swing.

**Directions:** Lie on your back with your knees bent and your arms at your side. Gently raise your hips (*fig* 11.40) and hold for 20 seconds.

## S26. Cobra

**Benefit**: This is an excellent stretch for the torso.

**Directions:** Lie prone on the floor with both forearms resting on the floor, slightly in front of your shoulders. Gently straighten your arms (*fig* 11.41), lifting your head and sternum up higher. Go easy here because this puts a lot of friction on your lower back. Relax your buttocks as you look up toward the sky. Hold for 5 seconds.

Static Stretch: Hold for 10 seconds.

11.41. Arms straightened.

## S27. Triangle

**Benefit**: This exercise works a multitude of the body's muscle groups at the same time. In addition to stretching the hamstrings, hips, chest, and lower back, the Triangle also stretches out the lats and obliques (on our sides), which allow the body to achieve a maximum torso turn and create arm extension. This is also great for helping to eliminate the chicken wing.

**Directions:** Stand against a wall with your feet slightly wider than shoulder width. Flare your right foot approximately 90 degrees in the direction you're going to lean. **If you have bad knees, keep your feet**

11.42. Press your hands, arms, shoulders and hips against the wall.

11.43. One arm dropped down with both arms against the wall.

**pointing straight ahead.** Flare your arms and hands directly out to your sides with your shoulders firmly against the wall (*fig* 11.42). Keep the backs of your hands, arms, and shoulders against the wall at all times. Slowly drop your lead arm down as far as you can without forcing it. Make sure your shoulders and arms stay pressed to the wall. *Don't* let either arm or shoulder come off of the wall. Slowly look up at the top arm, making sure it too is against the wall (*fig* 11.43). You'll feel this stretch in your lats (side muscles). Breathe deeply and fully with your ribs, and relax. Hold for 20 to 30 seconds on each side. It's not how far down you go that counts, but how deeply you breathe while maintaining the integrity of your posture

11.44. Extended lateral starting position.

11.45. Extended lateral ending position.

## S28. Extended Lateral

**Benefit**: This pose is excellent for developing function (mobility and stability) in your legs as well as creating bilateral hip activity on both sides of your torso. Like the Triangle, it increases range of motion in the muscles of your sides (lats and obliques), as well as developing strength in your legs, which will help create greater ease in trunk rotation and synchronize all of the body's major muscle groups.

**Directions:** Stand with your back against a wall with your arms extended and heels and buttock touching. Take your right foot, turn it parallel to the wall, and spread your feet about three to four feet sideways (*fig* 11.44). Your right foot should be 3 inches from the wall. Bend your right knee and lean your entire upper torso toward your right foot. Place your right arm on your right thigh. Raise your left arm over your head and look up toward the ceiling (*fig* 11.45). **Make sure that your shoulders and hips stay pressed against the wall.** Hold for 20 to 30 seconds. Repeat and do the other side.

*Secrets of Golf Instruction and Flexibility*

11.46. Hands holding ankles, arched backwards.

11.47. Right hand grabs right ankle and left arm extends forward.

## S29. The Bow

**Benefit**: This pose complements the Solo Sitting Wall (S18, p.175) by further stretching out the anterior muscles and contracting the posterior muscles.

**Directions:** Start by lying on your chest. Bend your knees and feet back toward your head. Grab each ankle with your hands and arch backwards (*fig* 11.46). Hold the pose for 20 seconds.

Many people will not be able to grab their ankles. If you can't, use a rope or stretch bands for assistance, or use the alternate Extended Half Bow (S29A below). Hold for 20 seconds.

## ALTERNATE (S29A): EXTENDED HALF BOW

**Benefit**: This is an excellent stretch that provides strengthening, flexibility, and extension to the core muscle group.

**Directions:** Lie supine on the floor. Take your right hand and grab your right ankle. Simultaneously, extend your left arm forward (*fig* 11.47). Now gently lift your right leg off the ground while you gently pull the right foot toward your head. At the same time, extend with the left arm while you're lifting your chest off of the floor. Hold for 15 to 20 seconds and repeat on the other side.

11.48. Seated with back straight.

11.49. Grasping chair and pulling body forward.

## S30. Seated Forward Bend

**Benefit**: This stretch warms up the muscles of the spine to prepare for the spinal twists to follow. Warming up the erector spinae muscles is important in allowing the spine to rotate during the golf swing.

**Directions:** Sit on the edge of a chair with your back straight (*fig* 11.48). Tuck your chin down and grasp the sides of your legs or the legs of the chair as you pull your body forward (*fig* 11.49). Hold for one to two seconds and come up. Breathe deeply and fully. Repeat 5 to 10 times.

## S31. Oblique Side Flexion

*WARNING: Do not do this posture if you have disc involvement.*

**Benefit:** Want a better shoulder turn? This exercise stretches your obliques, which will increase your trunk rotation on both sides of the ball.

**Directions:** Sit on the edge of a chair in an "upright" position (*fig* 11.50). Clasp your hands together and place them behind your head. Maintaining

*Secrets of Golf Instruction and Flexibility*

11.50. Seated with back straight.

11.51. Gently twist to one side.

11.52. Sink down toward floor.

your posture, inhale and gently twist to the left side (*fig* 11.51). Exhaling, lead with your right elbow and sink down toward the floor (*fig* 11.52). Try to keep your left elbow pointing up and behind you. Do not force this, but maintain your posture. Hold for two seconds and inhale back to the starting position. In other words, think "Upright Posture, Rotate, Down."Repeat and do the other side. Do 5 to 10 repetitions per side.

## SPINAL TWISTS

*WARNING: Use care or eliminate the following exercises if you have back problems or have been injured.*

## S32. Pretzel Stretch

**Benefit**: A stretch for the lower lumbar and obliques, this aids in developing a greater shoulder turn.

**Directions:** Sit on the floor with your legs extended and your back as straight as possible. Place your right foot just outside your left knee, making sure you keep the foot flat. Initially it doesn't matter how far up your leg you place your foot. Now, take your

11.53. Right hand is midline with your back; lift sternum.

11.54. Alternate Pretzel stretch.

right hand and place it directly behind the midline of your body. With your left arm straight, press it against your right thigh, just above the knee. Lift your sternum and look as far behind you as you can. Breathe deeply while pressing the left arm against the thigh (*fig* 11.53). Hold the pose for 30 to 45 seconds on each side.

### Alternate (S32A): Pretzel in Chair

An easier way to do the Pretzel is in a chair. Make sure that you keep your feet solidly on the ground as you twist (*fig* 11.54).

## S33. Upper Spinal Floor Twist

**Benefit**: The upper spine rotates approximately 60 to 70 percent more than the lower spine in the golf swing. When a person has rounded shoulders, this tightness inhibits the freedom of the shoulder turn. This pose stretches out and relaxes the anterior muscles in the upper chest and shoulders.

**Directions:** Lie on one side in a fetal position with your calves, thighs, torso, and arms at a 90-degree angle. Keep your knees pressed against a prop (*fig* 11.55). Place your arms straight out in front of you with your hands together, as if in prayer (*fig* 11.56). Take the top hand and arm, and slowly swing it all the way over to the other side toward the floor (*fig* 11.57). Keep the bottom hand on the floor, and make sure that you keep your knees pressed against the prop. Relax and notice that your extended hand, arm, and shoulder will begin to enter into deeper levels of relaxation, slowly getting closer to the floor. If your shoulders get sore, simply lower the arm closer to your torso to ease the torque. Hold each side for one minute.

*Secrets of Golf Instruction and Flexibility*

11.55. Keep your knees pressed against a prop.

11.56. Arms straight out with hands together.

11.57. Swing your top arm over, keeping your knees against the prop.

## S34. Crocodile

**Benefit**: Another great stretch for increasing your shoulder turn, this pose stretches the muscles of the spine as well as the obliques and also helps achieve maximum rotation of the thorax.

**Directions:** Lie on your back with your legs extended and your feet pointed straight up. Start by putting the heel of your right foot on top of the toes of your left foot. Extend your arms out to your sides with your palms facing down (*fig* 11.58). Keeping your legs tight and your feet arched back toward you, roll your hips and legs over to the left while pressing into the ground with your hands. The success of this pose depends on keeping your legs tight and your feet arched back. Don't worry if you can't get your feet to touch the ground. Turn your head to the right, countering the force of your hips (*fig* 11.59). Hold this position for one minute. Repeat and do the other side.

11.58. Arms out and palms facing down.

11.59. Head and right arm back to the right.

11.60. Rotate your trunk onto your shoulder.

11.61. Rotate to the other side.

## S35. Russian Ball Twist

Benefit: These twists will increase your core strength and improve your trunk rotation.

**Directions:** You'll need a physio ball for this stretch. Place your back, shoulders, and head on the ball. Lift your hips up so that they're in a straight line with your torso. Holding your arms straight up in front of you (vertical to the ground), clasp your hands together. Place your tongue on the roof of

11.62. Arms high.

your mouth. Begin rotating your trunk as far as possible to one side using a slow and deliberate tempo (*fig* 11.60 and *fig* 11.61). Hold for two seconds on the end of the exercise. Make sure to keep your hips up at all times.

Moderate workout: 5 to 10 repetitions.

Advanced workout: Increase repetitions, or do two to three sets of 5 to 10 repetitions.

## SHOULDERS

## S36. Overhead Extension

**Benefit**: This is an excellent opening warm-up stretch that oxygenates the entire body and prepares the muscles for the remainder of the protocol.

*Secrets of Golf Instruction and Flexibility*

**Directions:** Stand "at attention" (preferably against a wall). Keep your legs tight, and raise your arms as high as they'll go while keeping your shoulder blades pressed together (*fig* 11.62). Push your pelvis slightly forward. Don't force this stretch and remember to *breathe*. Hold for 10 seconds.

## S37. Pectoralis (Pec) Stretch

**Benefit**: This exercise stretches out the muscles of the chest and shoulders, which tend to shorten due to our forward-flexion culture. Stretching the anterior muscles of the shoulders allows you to expand the muscles on the backswing, making a freer and fuller shoulder turn.

**Directions:** Pec stretches can be done a number of ways. Standing with your feet shoulder width apart, place your arms at 8:00 and 4:00 and stretch them rearward (*fig* 11.63), holding for one to two seconds. Move your arms to 9:00 and 3:00 for one to two seconds (*fig* 11.64), and then move them up to 10:00 and 2:00 (*fig* 11.65) and hold for one to two seconds. Repeat each position three times.

11.63. Arms at 8:00 and 4:00.  11.64. Arms at 9:00 and 3:00.  11.65. Arms at 10:00 and 2:00.

11.66. In a doorway.

11.67. Using two chairs or props.

11.68. Golfer's grip.

### Alternate (S37A): Pec in Doorway

Another way to stretch the pecs is to use a doorway (*fig* 11.66) and allow your body weight to lean forward.

### Alternate (S37B): Pec with Chairs

Still another method is to use two chairs or props, get down on your knees, and place your forearms on each chair so that your knees are directly underneath your hips, and your arms are 90 degrees from your torso (*fig* 11.67). Gently lower your torso so you feel the stretch in your chest and shoulder blades. Don't force it, but rather concentrate on your breathing.

### S38. Arm Circles

**Benefit**: This stretch strengthens the muscles of the back while increasing range of motion in the shoulder sockets and creating greater freedom of the arms throughout the golf swing.

**Directions:** Stand erect with your chest lifted and your feet squared. With your arms hanging at your sides, place your hands with your fingertips curled inward and your thumbs outward (*fig* 11.68). We call this the "golfer's grip." Raise your arms out to your sides at shoulder level, parallel to the floor (*fig* 11.69). Keeping the shoulder blades pressed together, rotate the arms in approximately six-inch-diameter circles, gradually increasing the size of the circles. After approximately 10 circles, reverse directions and go the other way. Then turn up your palms to face the sky (*fig* 11.70) and circle backwards.

Try to do at least a total of 40 arm circles (20 frontward and 20 backward). You can increase this number as you see fit. Keep your shoulders back and your chest lifted at all times.

11.69. Arms at shoulder level.

11.70. Palms facing sky.

## S39. Elbow Curls

**Benefit**: This stretch engages the posterior muscles of the upper back, enhancing range of motion in the shoulder sockets, and creating greater freedom of the arms throughout the golf swing.

**Directions:** Using the golfer's grip (*fig* 11.68), place your knuckles against your temples with your upper arms parallel to the ground and your thumbs facing down. Keeping your arms horizontal to the ground,

11.71. Knuckles against temples and elbows touching.

11.72. Elbows extended to maximum position.

bring your elbows in toward each other until they touch (*fig* 11.71). (If they can't touch, then you have excessive tightness in your upper chest and shoulders.) Hold this position for one second, and then extend your elbows behind you until they come to their maximum position (*fig* 11.72). Repeat 10 to 20 times.

## S40. Why Me's

**Benefit**: This stretch increases range of motion in the pecs and shoulders.

**Directions:** Stand with your arms bent and your palms facing outward. Slowly lift with your elbows to shoulder height (*fig* 11.73) and raise your forearms to a position vertical to the ground. While lifting the arms, rotate the forearms and hands outward so that the palms face each other and the thumbs point backwards (*fig* 11.74). Hold for two seconds at the top of the movement and repeat 8 to 10 times.

11.73. Palms facing outward.

11.74. Forearms rotated, palms facing each other.

*Secrets of Golf Instruction and Flexibility*

11.75. Forearms parallel to the ground, fingers pointing toward chest.

11.76. Arms extended.

## S41. Breast Stroke

**Benefit**: This stretch increases range of motion in the pecs and shoulders.

**Directions:** Place your forearms parallel to the ground, hands together, with the fingers pointing toward your chest (*fig* 11.75). Roll the thumbs in towards your chest, and then extend your arms out as if you were doing a breaststroke in the pool (*fig* 11.76). Repeat 8 to 10 times.

## S42. Lateral Ball Rolls

**Benefits**: This stretch is powerful and improves many areas of the body at the same time, especially the posterior muscles of your back and shoulders.

**Directions:** Position your body so that your head is comfortably supported on the ball, as well as the area between your shoulder blades. Lift your hips so that they are in a straight line with your torso. Extend both arms out to the sides and keep your tongue on the roof of your mouth. Begin to roll laterally to the one side of the ball, keeping the alignment of your arms

11.77. Keep your hips in a straight line with torso.

11.78. Roll from side to side, keeping your arms parallel to the ground and hips elevated.

horizontal to the ground (*fig* 11.77). Start out slowly, eventually shuffling your feet to accommodate going further out on the edge of the ball (*fig* 11.78). As you progress with this exercise, you'll be able to support yourself with only one shoulder on the ball. Go slowly in the beginning until you build up to that point. As you end each side, hold the position for three seconds before rolling back to the other side.

Begin by doing 5 to 7 repetitions. Always warm up before doing this exercise. Slowly increase your repetitions as the exercise gets easier to do.

## S43. Internal & External Shoulder Rotators

**Benefit**: This stretch is for achieving more range of motion in the shoulder area, particular, the rotator cuff. These stretches will benefit people with tight or rounded shoulders. Loosening these muscles will help you achieve much greater freedom in your shoulder rotation.

### Internal Rotators

**Directions**: Stand upright with your chest lifted and your shoulders back. Raise your arms out to the sides so that your elbows are level with your shoulders and your palms and forearms are facing the ground (*fig* 11.79). Your arms should be at 90-degree angles to your torso and parallel to the ground. Hold and lock the angle of your elbows as you rotate your arms up

11.79. Place hands and arms parallel to the ground.

11.80. Rotate forearms upward.

11.81. Arms downward.

and back, so that they're over your head (*fig* 11.80). Hold for two seconds and return to the starting position and repeat.

For maximum stretch, do 8 to 10 repetitions.

## External Rotators

Begin in the same starting position as the internal rotators and repeat, only this time, with your arms downward (*fig* 11.81). Hold for two seconds and repeat.

For a maximum stretch, do 8 to 10 repetitions.

## S44. Head & Neck Stretches

*Caution: Don't do neck stretches until you've loosened up your hips and upper torso first.*

**Benefit**: These stretches allow maximum mobility of the upper back and neck. In the golf swing, flexibility in these muscles aids in allowing a free rotation of the cervical spine.

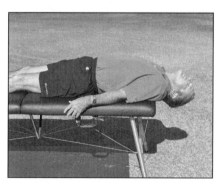

11.82. Head hanging over edge of table in starting position.

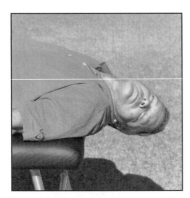

11.83. Head tilted to the left.

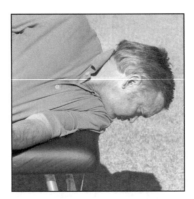

11.84. Turned onto side and looking down.

11.85. Sitting upright with chin down.

**Directions:** Lie on a bed or table with the tops of your shoulders and your head hanging over the edge (*fig* 11.82). Hold this position for 30 seconds to 1 minute. Then tilt your head all the way to the right for 15 seconds. Then tilt your head all the way to the left (*fig* 11.83) for 15 seconds. Turn and lie on one side with the top of your shoulder and head hanging over the edge. Look straight down (*fig* 11.84) for 15 seconds, then turn and do the same on the other side for 15 seconds. Lastly, sit upright on the edge of the table and tuck your chin down into your sternum (*fig* 11.85) for 15 seconds.

## CORE EXERCISES

### S45. Plank

**Benefit**: This core strengthening exercise develops strength throughout the entire torso. Having a strong core develops stability that goes hand in hand with the flexibility provided in the rest of the program.

**Directions:** Lie on your forearms with your entire body off the floor. Try to keep your hips level with your entire torso (*fig* 11.86). Make sure your breaths are even on the inhales and exhales. After some time, raise one leg while keeping the body propped up (*fig* 11.87). Hold for up to one minute. Then switch and do the same with the other leg.

11.86. Maintain a straight torso.

11.87. Plank with leg extension.

## Alternate (S45A): Advanced Plank

For a more advance version of the plank, straighten your arms (*fig* 11.88) and hold the position. Build up your time in this pose.

## S46. Wall Squats

**Benefit**: This stretch will help you achieve superb lower body stability in your golf swing by strengthening your legs and hips.

11.88. Advanced plank with straight arms.

**Directions:** You'll need a physio ball for this stretch. Stand with your back against the ball, supported by a wall. Keep your feet, knees, hips, and shoulders in line, making sure your feet are straight ahead (*fig* 11.89). Inhale, then squat down as you exhale (*fig* 11.90). Only go as low as comfortable. Don't let your knees go past your toes, and don't let your knees go outside or inside your feet.

11.89. Back against ball with feet straight ahead.

11.90. Squat down then back up.

Stand up, inhaling on the way up. **If you have soreness in your knees, be very careful and don't put too much pressure on them.** Do 1 to 10 repetitions. Build up the repetitions over time.

11.91. Exhale as you lift the head, chest, and legs.

11.92. Place hands behind the head for advanced stretch.

11.93. Using stretch bands for an advanced stretch.

### S47. Locust

**Benefit**: This pose develops a strong and elastic spine and is especially good for people with weak and tight backs.

**Directions:** Lie full length on the floor fully extended. Stretch the arms back with the palms facing up. Exhale and lift the head, chest, and legs off the floor simultaneously (*fig* 11.91). Contract the buttocks and stretch the thigh muscles. Keep both legs fully extended and the arms and feet off of the floor. Stay in this position as long as possible while breathing deeply and fully.

## Alternate (S47A): Advanced Locust

Clasp the hands around the back of the head (*fig* 11.92) and follow the instructions of Locust (S47 above).

## Alternate (S47B): Extended Locust

**Benefit**: This pose develops a strong and elastic spine and is especially good for people with weak and tight backs.

**Directions:** You'll need stretch bands for this stretch. Place the stretch bands under your feet and hold the other ends in your hands. Elongate your torso as much as possible while you lift your legs, chest, and arms off of the floor (*fig* 11.93). Hold for 20 seconds.

## RELAXATION POSES

### S48. Static Back Press

**Benefit**: This pose is extremely important because not only does it relax all the muscles throughout your body, especially the powerful hip flexors, it helps realign the joints of the body and restore its natural four-socket position.

11.94. Breathe deeply and relax.

**Directions:** Lie on your back with your knees up on a chair or block (*fig* 11.94). Keep your hands under your shoulders and simply relax. Make sure you breathe deeply by allowing the abdomen to expand outward as you inhale and back down on the exhale.

### S49. Supine Groin Stretch

**Benefit**: This stretch is very powerful for relaxing and lengthening the hip flexors. Our hips take a beating in our sitting-down culture and as a result, cause a multitude of health and fitness problems. When the hips get out of alignment, virtually every joint in the body is affected.

After practicing this pose, in time the joints of the body will begin to realign back into the four-socket position that nature intended. This pose will increase functionality and begin to eliminate the pain from misaligned joints.

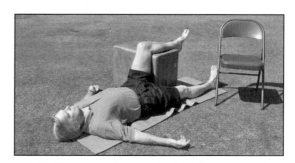

11.95. Elevate one leg on a block and support the foot of the straight leg with solid object.

**Directions:** Lie on your back with one leg bent on a chair or block and the other leg extended on the floor. Make sure that your extended foot is propped against something (*fig* 11.95). Simply relax and breathe fully and deeply with the diaphragm. In a short time, you'll begin to feel an easing of muscular tension. After you've spent time on one side, repeat and do the other leg.

Try to do an average of 10 to 15 minutes per side per session; even 5 minutes on each side will be of benefit. You can do up to 30 minutes a side. Because this pose is time consuming, I often recommend that people take one day a week off of your flexibility programs and do the pose for 30 minutes to even an hour per side. Although this may seem like a long time to do a pose, it will surely keep your hips relaxed for the entire week, thus, eliminating having to do the stretch daily.

11.96. Elevate one leg on chair or step ladder.

## Alternate (S49A): Supine Groin Stretch—Elevated Leg

An even better method is to use a small step ladder, chair, bookcase, or multiple positioning tower. Place the extended leg at an angle on a higher step or shelf, and allow the foot to rest upon it. As the lower back relaxes into the floor, begin to lower the extended leg down to the next level until it finally rests on the floor. In other words, if you were to spend 20 minutes per side, start with the foot on the fourth rung of the step ladder and hold for 5 minutes. After 5 minutes, drop the leg down to the third rung and hold for 5 minutes, etc. Or using a chair, place the foot elevated on the seat of the chair for 10 minutes, then down on the floor for 10 minutes (*fig* 11.96).

# S50. Supine Ball Rolls

*Warning: Do not do this stretch if you have back problems, especially disc involvement, as it puts stress on your lower back. As your back problems get better, begin to do this stretch under the supervision of a qualified person well versed in anatomical function.*

11.97. Slowly roll back and forth messaging the back.

**Benefit**: This is a fabulous stretch to lengthen your entire body and especially your abdomen, chest, and shoulders.

**Directions:** You will need a physio ball for this stretch. Lie on your back on a physio ball (*fig* 11.97). Slowly roll back and forth, getting a nice massage of the back. Do this for one minute. This pose counters the Solo Sitting Wall (S18 p.175) and further helps stretch the anterior muscle chains, while increasing stability in the posterior chains.

*Secrets of Golf Instruction and Flexibility*

# 12

# *What to Expect*

Nearly every one of my clients asks me "How long will it take before I see results?" Obviously, there is no one right answer simply because everybody is different and comes from a different level of anatomical function. However, for the average person, there are some common trends.

Most people begin to see improvements in the first few days, mainly that they're able to go further and deeper in the stretches, and they become easier to do. It's exciting when they see themselves improving. In around three weeks, most people notice more and more freedom in their bodies, and in their golf swings. As Arnold Palmer told me many times, "Something is happening to me. I feel lighter and taller." This brings up an interesting point. I've seen people regain up to two to three inches in height after embarking on the program. Do they actually grow? Of course not. Rather their muscles begin to elongate and come out of flexion. In other words, they begin to stand up straighter and taller because their tight muscles aren't pulling them forward in a rounded/hunchback posture.

The most noticeable improvement comes after two to three months, right around 90 days. Around this time, people's bodies and their golf swings begin to transform. Many of them literally have a glow about them and look more energetic and alive. The truth is they are more alive, simply because their bodies are more oxygenated. Their eyes actually have more sparkle. We are, after all, oxygen critters and desperately need oxygen to pervade our bodies. Depriving our bodies of oxygen for even a few minutes usually ends our life.

After nine months, people who have consistently maintained their programs have become different people. Their entire anatomical function has changed, for the better.

If you're not experiencing improvements, then be honest with yourself. Are you doing the program consistently? This program only works if you work it! Are you breathing deeply and fully? Are you doing enough of the programs?

If you've answered yes to these questions, then maybe there are some other things going on. How's your diet? If you're eating too much meat or junk food, your system will get clogged down, which will prevent the oxygen and blood flow from effectively getting into the nerve spindle and nerve fibers.

Are you doing too much weight lifting or running? Although resistance training and cardiovascular training is crucial, too much of a good thing can sometimes be a bad thing. Get checked out by a knowledgeable physical trainer who is versed in anatomical function. You also might want to see a good nutritionist.

If the muscles are receiving oxygen and blood and you're working the muscle chains properly, your muscles *must* expand more deeply. If not, look at what else you may be doing that may be impeding your progress.

I cannot express enough the importance of having fun and keeping a positive attitude about your programs. I want you to *expect* to improve and *know* that you're going to improve. A positive mind will produce positive results. I've seen a lot of people who had nothing wrong with them but didn't get results because of their negative attitude. I have been incredibly fortunate to have gotten to know and coach many of the greatest golfers, athletes, and business leaders, and I have yet to see one of them with a negative attitude. Not one! Those people are great because they set a goal and nothing was going to stop them. I want you to possess the same attitude. If you do, you'll be amazed before you're halfway through.

## THE JACK NICKLAUS INSPIRATION STORY

When on this topic, I always feel compelled to share this true story about the greatest golfer who ever lived.

One day Jack was in Pete Egoscue's clinic, and one of Pete's clients had his young son with him. Upon learning that Jack was in the clinic, the man asked Pete if his son could be introduced to Mr. Nicklaus and hopefully have Jack give him some words of wisdom.

As the introductions were made, Jack asked the boy what he liked to do. The boy responded that he loved to play golf and aspired to grow up and be a professional golfer "just like you, Mr. Nicklaus." Jack acknowledged him and then asked, "What else do you like to do, and what other sports do you play?" The boy replied that he really didn't play any other sports or do many other things, just golf.

Jack said, "Well, son, if that's the case, I would get off of that regimen of only playing golf, and get out there and also try other sports and do as many other things as you can. I highly recommend that you not *just* play golf." He then added, "And before you go expand your life, remember that life is short, and *the* most important thing you can do for yourself is to stay fit. After all, you can have all the money, power, pride, and prestige in the world, but if you don't have your health, you're a poor man." He then followed up by sharing how he had been successful but was encumbered by several physical ailments, and now, because he was taking more responsibility for his health, he was feeling great again. "So, son, my final advice for you is to keep yourself fit."

The boy didn't look like he got the message, but I can assure you, the rest of us standing in that room that day sure did!

I want to close this book by saying that there was a long time in my life when I didn't take care of myself and, as a result, I lived in pain. It's now been a long time since those days, and I can now say that I live pain free. I say without hesitation that feeling good is what it's all about! And for me it starts with flexibility. Speaking of feeling better, nothing makes me feel better than when I bump into people at the golf course, in restaurants, or wherever, and they stop me and share their positive testimonials of how these flexibility programs have changed their lives, improved their golf games, and changed their health for the better.

I hope you get on these programs, see these results for yourself, and hopefully one day we can meet, so *you* can make my day!

*Roger*

# *Index*

# *About the Author*

For over twenty years, ROGER FREDERICKS has been one of the most influential and true pioneers of the golf fitness movement, and is one of the few golf professionals who is an expert in both golf instruction and in physiology.

Roger has worked on the golf swings and bodies of over 20,000 golfers, which include over 60 tour professionals and 7 Hall of Famers. The creator of the smash hit infomercial "Roger Fredericks Reveals Secrets to Golf Swing Flexibility," he frequently travels around the country conducting golf outings, seminars, and speaking engagements.

Roger resides in San Diego, California where he conducts his Golf Instruction and Flexibility Programs.

*Secrets of Golf Instruction and Flexibility*

Stretch Rope.
Featured on page 168.

Slant Board.
Featured on page 172.

Swiss Exercise Ball.
Featured on page 188.

# *Essential Equipment Checklist*

The following list of equipment will help you get the most from the Drills and Stretches prescribed in this book:

- Stretch Rope

- Slant Board

- Swiss Exercise Ball

- Power Fan

- Impact Bag

You can find all of these items at Roger's website:

## **www.FredericksGolf.com**
## **or call**
### **888.304.FLEX (3539)**

Power Fan.
Featured on page 131.

Impact Bag.
Featured on page 131.

*Secrets of Golf Instruction and Flexibility*

*Also From Roger*